The Fifth Year of

THE

Nixon Watch

PREVIOUS BOOKS BY JOHN OSBORNE IN THIS SERIES

THE NIXON WATCH,
illustrated by Robert Osborn

THE SECOND YEAR OF THE NIXON WATCH,
illustrated by Bill Mauldin

THE THIRD YEAR OF THE NIXON WATCH,
illustrated by Pat Oliphant

THE FOURTH YEAR OF THE NIXON WATCH,
illustrated by Paul Conrad

The Fifth Year of
THE
Nixon Watch

BY

JOHN OSBORNE

Caricatures by DAVID LEVINE

LIVERIGHT

NEW YORK

LIVERIGHT

1.987654321

This book consists of articles that appeared in *The New Republic* between January 1973 and January 1974. The title is derived from "The Nixon Watch," the standing head under which John Osborne reports the Presidency for that magazine. Apart from some changes of tense for present clarity, the corrections of typographical errors, and the addition of updating addenda at the ends of a few chapters, the originals have not been altered for this publication. All the articles are reprinted by permission of the publisher.

ISBN: 0–87140–582–2
LC Number: 73–93125

Manufactured in the United States of America

CONTENTS

The Fifth Year of

T H E

Nixon Watch

I

Changing the Players

After four years of fussing with the structures and processes of the federal government, with particular attention to the White House organization at the top of it, Mr. Nixon said on January 5, in a statement which may be read as a restrained confession of miscalculation and deficiency in his first term, that one of his important purposes at the beginning of his second term is to get his administration in shape to "do a better job of managing the affairs of government over the next four years." His endeavor to accomplish this by means of reorganization, outright firings, accepted resignations, the reassignment of some officials and the recruitment of new ones isn't finished yet, six weeks after the President announced the start of it. But it is far enough along for an appraisal. My appraisal, no doubt influenced by a bias in favor of officials who care more about their use of power and responsibility than they do about the instruments of power, is that the latest Nixon exercise in governmental reform and invigoration has turned out to be considerably more substantial in terms of the number and sweep of the changes involved, and even less meaningful in terms of probable result, than I expected it to be when I characterized it in previous reports as a charade undertaken largely for public effect.

Between November 28, a day after the President declared his intention to imbue his approaching second term with the kind of "vitality and excitement" that "a second administration usually lacks," and December 22, when the carefully paced announcements of changes at Cabinet, sub-Cabinet, White House and bureau levels tailed off for a while, 57 resignations and retirements and 87 nominations, appointments and decisions to retain officials in their present positions were disclosed. Thirty nominations to jobs of sufficient importance to require Senate confirmation were sent to the 93rd Congress the day it convened. Six of the 11 departments got new secretaries. Three of these nominees were new to government, three were already in the administration. Five of the President's White House assistants were nominated to be departmental undersecretaries and assistant secretaries and agency heads. Elliot Richardson, the secretary of Health, Education, and Welfare, replaced Defense Secretary Melvin Laird. HEW's undersecretary, two assistant secretaries and four of its divisional administrators, including the entire directorate of its health services, were replaced. The secretary, an undersecretary, three assistant secretaries and two administrators left the Labor Department and Peter Brennan, a New York construction union leader, was installed at its head. James R. Schlesinger, chairman of the Atomic Energy Commission, replaced Richard Helms at the head of the Central Intelligence Agency. Kenneth Rush, the deputy secretary of Defense, moved to the State Department to be its deputy secretary under William P. Rogers, who is expected to stay another year or so and then resign. And so it went, in a swift realignment without remembered precedent in a transition from a reelected President's first term to his second term. Richard Nixon amply fulfilled and in early January was still fulfilling his promise to change "some of the players" on his team and thus combat what he called "the tendency . . . for an administration to run out of steam after the first four years and then to coast, and usually coast downhill." Without change on the scale he promised and proceeded to impose, he said,

both elected and appointed officials become "prisoners" of the
bureaucracy "they are supposed to run" and fail in their duty to
follow "the directions that the people want them to follow."

There can be no quarrel with the proposition that officials tend
to go stale in office, though Mr. Nixon would have vigorously
rebutted the argument if it had been applied to him in his bid for
a second term. But the observer of the Nixon exercise is entitled
to wonder whether the patent showmanship displayed in it doesn't
explain a lot of it and whether the obvious loss in continuity and
experience won't in the long run outweigh whatever gains in vigor
and fresh outlook the President may get from it all. Elliot Richardson, for instance, indicated when his transfer from HEW to Defense was announced that he would have preferred to stay awhile
with the organizational monster that he had been slowly mastering
since he took charge of it in 1970. It's understood that he could
have remained at HEW if he had insisted. But he is sufficiently
versed in the ways and quirks of Mr. Nixon to know that he would
have been in for an unhappy time if he had insisted. The President
resents and does not forget resistance to his wishes in such matters,
and Richardson is said to have understood that the real choice
before him was to move over to Defense, as Mr. Nixon asked, or
to leave the public service. Kenneth Rush, the deputy secretary
of Defense, similarly indicated that he would have preferred to
become secretary of Defense instead of deputy secretary of State.
He gave an impression that he complied with the President's wish
in much the same spirit of doubting obedience that prevailed in
Elliot Richardson's case.

Two brief passages in a lengthy message on governmental reorganization that the President sent to Congress in March 1971
justify a more serious doubt that the reasoning behind Mr. Nixon's
approach to government is as sound and thoroughly thought out
as he makes it appear to be. This was the message in which he
proposed to consolidate seven federal departments and the functions of several independent agencies into four "goal-oriented"
departments of Human Resources, Natural Resources, Community
Development and Economic Affairs. It was and still is the President's major attempt to bring into "the affairs of government"
that condition of ordered neatness and precision which he yearns

and strives to attain. He has said that he will ask a hitherto indifferent Congress to enact his great consolidation, with some revisions, at the 1972–73 session. The two passages that invite doubt and wonder have the President saying that "good people cannot do good things with bad mechanisms" and that "the major cause of the ineffectiveness of government is not a matter of men or money. It is principally a matter of machinery."

Now, it may be presumptuous of a journalist to question the managerial wisdom of a President who has been in and out of public office since 1946 and of the array of organizational experts —chief among them Roy Ash, the former president of troubled Litton Industries and Mr. Nixon's new director of the Office of Management and Budget—who devised the consolidation. But the quoted passages suggest to me that Mr. Nixon and his experts, notably Mr. Ash, let their preoccupation with the "machinery" blind them to the nature and purpose of government. Good people do good things with bad mechanisms all the time. If they didn't and couldn't, the federal government would be in sadder shape than Mr. Nixon supposes it to be. Whether government is effective or ineffective is not "principally a matter of machinery." It is a matter of the will, or lack of will, of the people who head and run government, beginning of course with the President, to recognize the needs of the society and to provide the measures and means, including money, that must be provided if the needs are to be met. Preoccupation with machinery, in the degree that Mr. Nixon is preoccupied with it, can be a cover for inability or unwillingness to recognize and face up to and meet the needs.

Mr. Nixon has just disclosed a scheme to accomplish part of his departmental consolidation by executive fiat and action. He is giving three of his Cabinet secretaries (Earl Butz at Agriculture, James T. Lynn at Housing and Urban Development, Caspar Weinberger at HEW) the added titles and prestige of counsellors to the President, installing them across the way from the White House, and charging them with coordinating policy formulation and, to some extent, departmental administration in the areas of natural resources, community development and human resources. Mr. Nixon has tried the same approach twice before, with White House assistants doing the coordinating, and it hasn't worked to the President's satisfaction. He seems to think it will, this time. What I need, I reckon, is his faith in machinery.

January 20, 1973

―――――――

The consolidation by fiat faded away within months. Counsellors Butz, Lynn and Weinberger, never having accomplished much as counsellors, returned to their departments, and Congress did nothing about statutory consolidation.

The FTC's Future

Somebody at the White House, close enough to the President to be heeded by his press staff, understood on the morning of January 10 that Mr. Nixon wanted it to be generally understood that he accepted the resignation of Miles W. Kirkpatrick, the chairman of the Federal Trade Commission, without regret. On the available evidence, including a letter to Kirkpatrick in which the President said he was accepting the resignation "with deep regret" and "with special appreciation for your service," the somebody who instructed Deputy Press Secretary Gerald Warren to say precisely and only that the chairman's resignation was accepted "with appreciation for his contributions over the past years" was mistaken. But it was an authoritative mistake, revealing something more than the "failure of communication" within the White House labyrinth to which it was attributed after Warren took the blame on himself and apologized to Chairman Kirkpatrick for refusing, in answer to a reporter's question, to add some expression of presidential regret to the cold and minimal statement of "appreciation." It revealed, for one thing, the mechanical way in which the process of cleaning out the first-term Nixon administration in readiness for the second term was conducted by the assistants who draft the acceptances of resignations and determine the tone, ranging from no regret and no appreciation whatever to deep regret and profound appreciation, that the President's spokesmen are told to strike in announcing departures. More importantly, the soured announcement reflected the distaste of some of the President's principal assistants for the kind of reformist activism that has recently prevailed at the commission and their impression that Mr. Nixon doesn't like it any more than they do.

Whether the President likes it or not is less important than whether he now proposes to kill off the activism and let the FTC subside into the sodden condition it was in when he took office in 1969. The first indication came with his choice of Lewis A. Engman, a lawyer on the White House staff, to succeed Miles Kirkpatrick. There is precedent for placing a White House assistant on the commission—President Eisenhower did it in 1956—but not for designating a White House appointee to be chairman of the commission. At a time when President Nixon is striving to strengthen his command and control of the executive departments and agencies and centralize the making of federal policy in the White House, a natural and widespread reaction was bound to be that the choice of Lewis Engman signified an intention to extend presidential command and control to the theoretically independent regulatory agencies, beginning with the FTC. It is difficult to associate Nixon command and control with the vigorous policing of the market that the FTC attempted under Kirkpatrick, to the intense annoyance and discomfort of some of the President's most formidable corporate and individual constituents. At the risk that is always inherent in any grant of good faith to Richard Nixon, I nevertheless advise caution in jumping to the obvious conclusion to be drawn from the Engman nomination.

Very little is known of Engman himself, except that he is 37 years old; a lawyer from Michigan; a product of Harvard Law School and the London School of Economics; and, at the White House, by turns the general counsel of the President's Office of Consumer Affairs and one of six assistant directors of the Domestic Council under John D. Erlichman, the assistant for domestic affairs. The usual adjectives—bright, ambitious, aggressive—are applied to him by his White House associates. Miles Kirkpatrick, who had some dealings with Engman at the Office of Consumer Affairs, said of him, "I've got a high regard for his capacities. I think he's a fine lawyer. He would make a good commission chairman." Robert Pitofsky, who brought the FTC's Bureau of Consumer Protection to a high pitch of vigor and effectiveness under Kirkpatrick and quit on January 16 to return to New York University's law school faculty, said before the nomination was announced that he had found Engman to be genuinely concerned for consumer welfare. Pitofsky may be expected to wait awhile before suggesting to his law students that they go to work for the FTC in the new regime. But he didn't seem disposed to write off the commission's future in consumer advocacy and protection just because a Nixon assistant was to be the new chairman.

Miles Kirkpatrick's record and background suggest that charitable caution is in order. When the President chose him in 1969 to oversee an American Bar Association study of the commission and its flaws, there was reason to expect a whitewash in rebuttal to a devastatingly critical study that Ralph Nader had sponsored. Kirkpatrick was a prominent antitrust lawyer, his clients included a good many defendants in FTC proceedings, and the penetrating report that his study produced astonished the cynics. They were far from persuaded that a corporate lawyer with his record, the ABA study aside, would or could turn out to be the foe of market rascals and monopolists that he proved to be in the chairmanship. At a farewell press conference, the day after the announcement of his resignation was botched, Kirkpatrick touched upon one of the reasons why an FTC chairman can be as independent as he chooses to be, regardless of his antecedents. He said: "We continue to be independent, we should be independent, and we are a very important force because we are independent. Anybody coming here, any selection that the President would make, I cannot expect to be other than independent." Allowing for some judicious exaggeration, there is a sound basis for that observation.

The basis for it is that the FTC is independent by law, responsible to Congress rather than the President to the extent that it is responsible to any other authority. A chairman of the FTC is designated by the President from the five commission members and he serves as chairman, though not as member, at the President's pleasure. But, given a chairman with the intent and courage to preserve his and the commission's independence and to ward off the pressures that always endanger it, the countervailing pressures toward independence are substantial. No lawyer wants to be known among his fellows at the bar as a stooge, for Presidents or for corporate and other private interests. The internal pressures at the commission, from other members and particularly from the lawyers, economists and other specialists who staff it, are predominantly for movement and action rather than for inertia. This last is true now, at least, with a staff that has been drastically weeded out and freshened with new and reformist talent since Kirkpatrick took over in 1970. His predecessor and Mr. Nixon's first appointee as chairman, Caspar Weinberger, actually began the weeding out and restaffing, a fact that contributes to the feeling at the FTC that the advent of a certified Nixon man doesn't necessarily mean an end to vigor and reform.

Such are the possible plusses, reported as they are heard at the FTC. The minuses, rooted in a doubt that this President is capable of letting the FTC go its recent way without hindrance and suppression, are also substantial. One of them is that Mr. Nixon has two more vacancies on the commission coming up in 1973. Another is that most of the key staff appointees who make or break the work and effectiveness of the commission are leaving with or soon after Kirkpatrick. They include Robert Pitofsky in the consumer bureau, Alan Ward in antitrust, Michael Mann in the important Bureau of Economics and Executive Director Basil Mezines, a career man who is retiring this summer and who thinks with some reason that I unjustly tagged him as a channel of undue White House and private interference with the commission's work in a couple of pieces I wrote about the FTC in October 1971. The new chairman, Lewis Engman, will be principally responsible for replacing them. An early test of his intent and courage, and of the freedom the President is inclined to allow him or he insists upon, will be the replacements he chooses.

We close with a saddening note on the manner of Miles Kirkpatrick's going. The President could have found time to telephone and say he was sorry about the chill announcement. He didn't.

January 27, 1973

———

Chairman Engman's performance (and the commission's perfor-mance) in 1973 justified the confidence rather timidly indicated in the foregoing report.

III

Four Days

So there he was, at high noon on the first of the four days that launched him and the country upon his second four years, sedate and assured and somehow a harder and colder man than he appeared to be when he, at his first inaugural, promised to listen "to the injured voices, the anxious voices" in the land and lead us all "forward together . . . black and white together as one nation, not two." Richard Nixon at his second beginning in 1973 had no word for or about the injured and the anxious, except that the voices were quiet now and all Americans must forego the "false promise" of governmental solutions for all their problems and "do more for themselves" and ask "not just what government will do for me, but what can I do for myself?" Here was confirmation, boldly offered, that he was turning away from the course that he set forth in 1969 when he said: "In pursuing our goals of full employment, better housing, excellence in education; in rebuilding our cities and improving our rural areas; in protecting our environment and enhancing the quality of life—in all these and more, we will and must press urgently forward." The word in 1973, to be spelled out in the budget and State of the Union messages soon to

come, was that "Just as building a structure of peace abroad has
required turning away from old policies that have failed, so building a new era of progress at home required turning away from old
policies that have failed."

There on the Capitol plaza, with the flags at half mast for Harry
Truman and a cold wind blowing, the cold word was of course
that the President was not really turning away abroad or at home
but projecting "a better way to peace" and "a better way to progress." It could be so: he was soon to announce, on the fourth
of the days here recounted, that the Vietnam war was indeed
"coming to an end," and a source of Mr. Nixon's stolid assurance
must have been the remarkable shortage of dissent from his proposition that many of the federal social programs that he was about
to dismantle or at the least rearrange had not worked as they were
supposed to work and had not adequately served the purposes
that his predecessors since the time of Franklin Roosevelt had
expected them to serve. Nobody could dispute his boast that in
Peking and Moscow he had established "the base for a new and
more durable pattern of relationships among the nations of the
world" and it was possible that "a new era of peace in the world"
was at hand. Nobody was disposed to question, either, his statement that "the central question before us is: How shall we use
that peace?" and, in that moment of promise and confidence, Mr.
Nixon's determination to use it well.

Then came the drive back to the White House, with a few eggs
thrown at the presidential car and a few shouts and a few arrests,
but all shielded and remote from the counterinaugural staged by
some 60,000 haters of war at the Washington Monument. The
President had spent four years teaching them that they might as
well shut up and stay home, and he had succeeded beyond his
hopes in convincing his quiescent majority that the rebellious young
and disbelieving had nothing to teach him about the blessings of
peace and the way to it. The assurance in his own mind that this
was so, that the majority and the power that only it could give him
were now securely his, must have had something to do with his
ebullient and happy emergence that night at six inaugural balls—
he kept saying he couldn't remember whether it was five or six or
seven—from the seclusion in which he had largely enwrapped
himself since his reelection. "So here we go," he said at three of

the balls, announcing at each of the six that he was dancing with Mrs. Nixon and with other ladies (10 girls at one of them, by his count) for the first time since he as Vice President shared President Eisenhower's first inaugural in 1953. He kept it up from 10:30 P.M. until after 1 A.M., spewing gladsome banalities at the six jamborees and plainly getting his share of the money's worth from the $4 million that the entire celebration had cost the 30,000 people who paid anywhere from $10 to $1000 for admission.

Mr. Nixon, reinaugurated and refreshed, said on Sunday morning in the East Room that "it is a very great pleasure to welcome all of you who have come to this special inaugural service," and it must have been. There were some 300 of them, supporters and campaign and inaugural workers, and three divines who were to deliver "homilies": Rabbi Edgar F. Magnin from Los Angeles, the Reverend Billy Graham, and the Catholic Archbishop of Cincinnati, the Most Reverend Joseph L. Bernardin. Rabbi Magnin concluded with "We are fortunate indeed to have a great leader as our President—a modern Joseph. God bless you, Mr. President, and your dear family. God bless America!" Mr. Nixon's dear friend Billy Graham ended with: "Mr. President, I speak for the overwhelming majority of the American people when I say, 'God bless you, and God bless America!' " Archbishop Bernardin seemed to have set himself to answer the President's complaint in his inaugural address that "at every turn we have been beset by those who find everything wrong with America and little that is right." The archbishop said to Richard Nixon and the others in his presence that "our loss of self-confidence and self-assurance"— a loss that the President had recovered from if he had ever suffered it—should be taken as "a sign of growing maturity, stemming from a greater sense of realism" rather than the challenge Mr. Nixon perceived to "our faith in ourselves and in America." The real and compelling challenge, Archbishop Bernardin said, was "to strive, without respite, for justice and peace here and now, justice especially for the poor and the oppressed at home and abroad." Reporters who were there said that the President heard this with every show of respect and humility.

On the Monday, the President sent Henry Kissinger off to Paris for what proved to be a last, ceremonial session with Le Duc Tho of North Vietnam. The President was awaiting word of Kissinger's arrival in Paris and the world was awaiting the completion of an agreement to end the war in Vietnam and perhaps in all of Indochina when H. R. Haldeman, the White House chief of staff, was told by telephone from Texas and then told Mr. Nixon that Lyndon Johnson had been found dead of a heart attack in his bedroom at the Johnson ranch. How the President reacted was cloaked in the privacy that customarily surrounds him. It took two hours for the staff to draft and issue the President's statement that "No man had greater dreams for America than Lyndon Johnson" and that "Even as we mourn his death, we are grateful for his life." Twenty-six hours later, millions were to see on television that the President's lips trembled and that he swallowed briefly, as if choking back deep and true sorrow, when he referred to the dead President. Mr. Nixon must have been aware that some of his listeners would recall that in 1966 Lyndon Johnson had referred to him in anger and contempt as "a chronic campaigner" and that he, in his second inaugural rejection of "old policies that have failed," had just announced his intent to reconstruct if not to bury much of the Johnsonian Great Society. And he must have been aware, too, that the accounts and reminiscences of the large and gutsy President who was gone would invite cruel comparison with the crimped and cautious personality that Richard Nixon, with all of his escalations and deescalations of manner and tone, persists in projecting for himself.

Then came, with a curious lack of any sense of triumph, the President's announcement on the evening of the fourth day of his second beginning that "we today have concluded an agreement to end the war and bring peace with honor in Vietnam and in Southeast Asia." Six times in the speech, twice in one paragraph, the President referred to "peace with honor" and "an honorable agreement." There was no mention of the 12 days of savage bombing in December that had preceded and—Henry Kissinger was soon to imply—had brought about the final and conclusive round of negotiation in Paris. "Now that we have achieved an honorable agreement," the President said, "let us be proud that America did not settle for a peace that would have betrayed our allies, abandoned our prisoners of war, or that would have ended the war for us but would have continued the war for the 50 million people of Indochina." Eleven minutes after he began, the President was done and, according to his press spokesman, retired to the Lincoln Sitting Room in the White House mansion. Was he with his family? The spokesman didn't know. Was he celebrating in any fashion, except by—it was rather hesitantly said—telephone calls to and from members of his staff? The spokesman didn't know. Mr. Nixon had recently said in an interview that the triumphant moments such as his landslide reelection in November somehow faded off and left him rather deflated. So we in the White House press room were left with the television sets darkened or back on an all-star basketball game and Ed Sullivan, parading a batch of faded electronic stars. We were free to imagine the President in subdued reflection, sharing whatever doubts he may have had about the endurance and worth of his honorable peace only with people— attendants and family—who would not then or ever encourage doubt.

He had said in his speech that we'd get the English texts of the Vietnam agreements and protocols, and a briefing from Henry Kissinger the next day. We did, and this account of the four days must end without time for measured appraisal of them and of Kissinger's long exposition and justification of them. A few facts about them and about the prelude to them may be safely noted, however. The agreement does not give the President the "internationally supervised cease-fire throughout Indochina" that he set forth as one of his unalterable conditions on January 25 and May 8 of last year. The substantive differences between the agreement that he could have had at the end of October and the one that goes into effect on January 27 are few and hard to value, against the cost in lives and international repute that the country and its victims must pay and have paid for the December bombing. They are few enough, one noted at the Kissinger briefing, that Kissinger relapsed at the end from masterly justification of the Nixon course and exit into a tone of strained and anguished defense. He said: ". . . it should be clear by now that no one in the war has had a monopoly of anguish and that no one in these debates has had a monopoly of moral insight. And now that we have achieved an agreement . . . together with healing the wounds in Indochina, we can begin to heal the wounds in America."

Yet there is peace of a kind, in Vietnam and prospectively in Laos and maybe, just maybe according to Henry Kissinger, in Cambodia. The time of unwinnable war that the country and Indochina and the world have lived with for 10 years is at the least suspended for a while. The President leaves North Vietnam and its allies, Communist China and Soviet Russia, with the threat that the suspension may not really be an end to American intervention and military action if the ambiguous and fluid terms are violated. What shall we do with the peace?, the President asked in his second inaugural. That, fortunately, is not for him alone to answer.

February 3, 1973

———

What we got, it turned out, was not an end of the Vietnam war, with or without honor, but an end only to American military involvement. Even that, in Cambodia, was six months coming and then only at the will and insistence of Congress.

IV

Games with Topsy

Before getting to the main business of the day in the White House press room on January 26, Press Secretary Ronald Ziegler threw his engaging smile at the assembled reporters and said that he "would like to make one or two points, points that have perhaps not been presented clearly enough in the past."

When Ziegler introduces his remarks in that tone of implied apology for past derelictions, a reasonable assumption is that he has been told by H. R. Haldeman, the assistant in charge of White House management and in ultimate charge of a great deal else, including the care and improvement of the Nixon image, to get out there and set those jerks in the media straight on any line of news reporting and comment that may, at a given moment, be vexing Haldeman and his only superior in the White House hierarchy, the President. Ziegler's remarks on this occasion indicated that the President and Haldeman were vexed by the tendency of reporters and commentators to harp on a point that Mr. Nixon himself had made in the following words on November 27: "The White House staff has grown rather like Topsy. It has grown in every administration. It is now time to reverse the growth . . ." Arguing that the President was right and the journalists were wrong when he and they said in different ways that the White House staff had grown like Topsy during the Nixon years was a difficult assignment. But, for reasons that can be explained only by dragging the reader through a morass of figures and bureaucratic technicalities, the press secretary was able to sustain his argument with less deception than he is capable of practicing when he is ordered or chooses to do so.

The irritation that Ziegler reflected dates back to the first weeks of the Nixon tenure in early 1969 (when I, for example, wrote that Mr. Nixon had already installed "the biggest and most elaborate array of assistants, assistants to assistants, councils and sub-councils in presidential history"). The suffering in and near Mr. Nixon's Oval Office was acute in early 1973 because reports of this kind made it appear that the President was undoing what he had done in his first four years when he had his press spokesman and Roy Ash, the new director of the Office of Management and Budget, announce his first moves to chop down both his immediate staff and the staffs of the catch-all Executive Office of the President. "I think it is important," Ziegler said on the 26th, "that we put that into perspective. We are not decreasing an increase that has been put into effect by this administration . . . I keep seeing stories that during the Nixon administration, or [an interesting change!] during President Nixon's administration, the White House staff has been increased or the Executive Office of the President had been doubled. That is incorrect." The thrust of the press secretary's frequently repeated statements to the same effect was that what he called "the White House staff itself, the President's personal staff" had not increased at all and was being reduced from 147 functional assistants last November to around 90 by mid-1973. As for total employment in the encompassing Executive Office, it had decreased from 4700 in June of 1968 to 4250 in June of 1972 and would be cut to under 2000 by June of 1973.

How this last was to be accomplished was the meat of the news that Roy Ash was trotted out to announce after two hours of coaching by a team of White House publicists. They went to such lengths to prepare him because his few previous appearances before the

White House press and the White House staff had encouraged an impression that Director Ash, whatever his talents in management and organizational reform may be, is an unsurpassed mumbler of meaningless profundities when he seeks to enlighten people in groups. Either the coaching was marvelously effective or the impression was false. He dealt crisply and clearly with the President's plans to remove 389 employees from the Executive Office payroll by abolishing the moribund National Aeronautics and Space Council, shifting the advisory functions of the Office of Science and Technology to the National Science Foundation, and transferring the responsibilities of the Office of Emergency Preparedness for disaster relief, civil survival during nuclear attack, imports that might affect national security, and oil imports policy to the Department of Housing and Urban Development, the General Services Administration and the Treasury. Ash also confirmed without announcing the President's intention—Congress willing, which is uncertain—to abolish the federal government's central antipoverty agency, the Office of Economic Opportunity, and thereby accomplish most of the promised cut of some 2200 in the Executive Office rosters. Excepting the space council, for which there has never been much demonstrable need, there are good arguments against the changes and grounds for suspecting that a major purpose is simply to give the presidential establishment the lean and efficient look that Mr. Nixon desires. It must be acknowledged, however, that Roy Ash earned respect when he said, with the zeal of a true believer in organizational magic, that the purpose of these and forthcoming changes is to limit "the realm of the President's office to policy making" and to "preserve its special perspective, its special strength to determine policy, to assign responsibilities, to coordinate interagency activities and to oversee all agency operations." With his reference to overseeing "all agency operations," he certainly hit the mark. Strengthened presidential oversight and command of all federal activities, with the command centered at the White House, is the primary purpose of the entire second-term exercise in organizational reform.

And now, with appropriate shudders, back to the Nixon-Ziegler numbers game. The President's spokesman sustained his argument that there really has been no increase in "the White House staff, the President's personal staff" by sticking strictly to two entities, the Executive Office of the President and a unit within it that is called "the White House Office." This last is indeed the core of the President's staff. It is approximately true that the recent level of White House Office employment cited by Ziegler—510 authorized permanent employees, representing an actual total of about 600 and including clerical and other "support" personnel in addition to the functional assistants—is about what it was in 1968. But there's a catch: the larger Executive Office embraces five presidential offices and councils (telecommunications policy, domestic affairs, drug abuse, economic controls, environmental quality) that didn't exist in 1968. All of them are staffed and all of them serve the President in staff capacities. In December, they employed 550 functional assistants and supporting personnel. Their staffs are being reduced, along with the White House Office staff, but in mid-1973 they still will add some 450 White House employees to the authorized and publicized total of 480 White House Office employees. It is in these new Nixon offices and councils, and in Henry Kissinger's National Security Council, with a staff that has doubled since 1968 and is to be reduced very little if at all, that the White House establishment has grown "rather like Topsy" since Mr. Nixon took over.

Thirty of the 47 White House Office assistants who quit that staff in November and December got other government assignments. Four of them actually remained on the overall Nixon staff, at the Office of Management and Budget and with the Council on International Economic Policy. The reduction of 389 resulting from abolition of the space council, the Office of Science and Technology and the Office of Emergency Preparedness meant a net cut of only 66 in federal employment because OEP's 323 "permanent" employees are to be transferred to the agencies taking on its functions. Two of several White House Office assistants who haven't quit yet but are going to are Dwight Chapin, the President's appointments man, and Herbert Klein, the director of communications. The circumstances of their impending departures attest to the sour atmosphere that prevails at the Nixon White House behind the show of happy progress toward lean efficiency. Chapin is leaving because of his uncomfortably close association with the sabotage and other skullduggery that marred the Nixon campaign for reelection. Klein, who has served the President since the 1950s, has been invited out in order to clear the way for a planned reorganization and concentration of the entire White House news and propaganda operation under Ronald Ziegler. Working for Mr. Nixon these days isn't quite the fun it was when it all started four years ago.

February 10, 1973

———

I was not free to write at the time that Haldeman had referred to "those jerks in the media" in a then-current staff memo.

V

How It Works

The reporters who accompanied the President from Washington to California on February 8 wanted to know on the morning of Monday, February 12, why he had decided to return to Washington that afternoon instead of staying, as he had said he would, at the Western White House in San Clemente at least until midweek and probably until early the following week. An irritated journalist barked at Press Secretary Ronald Ziegler, "Did anyone ask him why?" and Ziegler answered: "I asked why. He said, 'Because I want to go back at 4 o'clock.' He could have said, 'I am going back for a specific reason,' but he didn't. That is why I have told you there is no specific reason I would point to. That is how it works."

And that indeed is how it often works, notwithstanding the common difficulty of believing that Presidents ever do anything for trivial and personal reasons. Mr. Nixon's second devaluation of the dollar was announced in Washington while he was flying back, and he had his picture taken with Treasury Secretary George Shultz the next morning. The logical and favored supposition was

that the President had concluded that it wouldn't look well for him
to be way off there in California while the American dollar was
sinking in the world money markets and this and other extreme
measures were being taken and prepared to improve the country's
deteriorating international trade situation. But, according to Secretary Shultz, the President decided upon devaluation two days before he made his choice between going to his home in California
and his home in Florida and left on six hours' notice for San
Clemente. He kept in telephone touch with Shultz and, as Ziegler
said in San Clemente, "he doesn't have to go back to Washington
to conduct economic conversations." A radio address to the nation
preceding a message to Congress on environmental protective measures could have been made as easily from San Clemente as from
Washington. On the President's first day back at the Washington
White House, an establishment that he increasingly seems to consider more a fortress than a home, he remarked with pleasure that
the weather was better in the capital than it was in California and
said, with some injustice to his home state, that "it was really cold
out there."

The power of presidential whim, a factor in affairs that has
mightily multiplied since the voters in 49 of the 50 states chose
Richard Nixon in preference to George McGovern last November,
was illustrated by the appearance in San Clemente of Caspar Weinberger, the President's third secretary of Health, Education, and
Welfare and the last of his second-term Cabinet nominees to be
confirmed by the Senate. Weinberger arrived in an air force Jetstar
on Sunday night and took his oath in Mr. Nixon's presence Monday morning, shortly after the President's intention to go back at
4 o'clock because he wanted to go back at 4 o'clock was announced. The President made occasion to congratulate himself
upon choosing in Weinberger a man of "great intelligence" and
"great compassion" who "believes in solving problems" and "does
not believe in wasting money in solving problems." Queried on
the cost of Weinberger's fast shuttle from and back to Washington,
Press Secretary Ziegler said with airy indifference that the flight
cost of a Jetstar probably runs to $600 or maybe $625 an hour.
To a President who on his own trip to California had just made his
first flight in a new Boeing jet acquired at a cost of $10 million,
this was peanuts.

Mr. Nixon said at a press conference on January 31 that he wasn't going to exploit the coming release of American prisoners of war by the North Vietnamese. It was a wise and decent decision and he stuck to it, while missing no chance in Washington and California to proclaim again and again his conviction that the majority of Americans, excepting "so-called better people" who persisted in criticizing his Vietnam policy, shared his belief that he had achieved "peace with honor." Watching the televised arrival of the first prisoners in the Philippines, I figured that the President would get into the act somehow without breaking his pledge to stay out of it, and he did when Colonel Robinson Risner, a pilot who was shot down and captured in 1965, telephoned the Western White House from Clark Field and said he wanted to speak to Mr. Nixon. The result was a happy and quickly publicized conversation in which Colonel Risner told the President that "all of the men would like to meet you personally to express their gratitude" and the President got a chance to refer once again to "an honorable end to the Vietnam situation." Ronald Ziegler explained the event as follows: "Let me emphasize this: Colonel Risner initiated the call on his own . . . There was no prior discussion with us about the fact that he was going to initiate the phone call. The phone call came in . . . and the President said, 'I want to return the call. I would like to talk with him if he is calling.' That is how it came about."

At the White House to which the President returned, his staff was in the process of getting through and over a feeling that his wants had more to do with whether they did or didn't remain in his service for the second term than their past services and loyalty to him did. A senior assistant who survived the reorganization and modest reduction of the staff that Mr. Nixon initiated the day after he was reelected acknowledged with unusual candor that he and his associates had been put through "a very low period" and were just beginning to recover some of the zest and confidence that they previously had and that they had expected the Nixon victory to enhance rather than diminish. A good deal of private pain and some tragedy attended the transition. A case in point, complicated by the continuing effort to preserve the President from any evidence that he could have had anything to do with or known about the burglary, spying and political sabotage that occurred during his

campaign for reelection, is that of Mr. Nixon's appointments secretary and devoted assistant, Dwight Chapin. I, for instance, recently reported as fact that Chapin is leaving the staff for a job
with United Airlines because of his inability to deny some involvement in the disgraceful campaign proceedings. Yet I'm told by
trusted White House friends that Chapin really was looking for a
private job before the scandal stories began to break last summer.
I believe it, but I also have to believe that Chapin's departure has
been welcomed if not demanded by the President and his stern
and reticent chief of staff, Bob Haldeman.

A typical victim of another sort is Peter M. Flanigan, who recently suffered a required removal from the prestigious West Wing
of the White House, where the President has his principal office,
to the adjoining Executive Office Building. Peter Flanigan is that
rare White House type, a very senior assistant who will admit it
when he becomes a bit less senior. When he was told that the question of what the office move meant was bound to arise and was
asked what he'd say it meant, he replied: "Sure. It means that
while I'm still an assistant to the President, my responsibilities
aren't as broad as those that George Shultz [who doubles as Treasury secretary and White House assistant], John Ehrlichman and
Henry Kissinger have. In this somewhat Byzantine town, it probably indicates that there's a difference among assistants to the
President." Flanigan is completing a study of what to do about
the nation's developing shortages of coal, oil and natural gas. As
director of the Council on International Economic Policy, he is
neck-deep in formulation of the President's plans to toughen up
tariff and other protective trade measures. All of that, he says with
every show of content, is enough to keep any one man busy and
in fair fettle.

The new occupant of Flanigan's previous West Wing office is
Kenneth Cole, aged 35, a comer and riser in the Nixon power-
house. He recently succeeded John Ehrlichman, the still-ascendant
assistant for domestic affairs, as director of the Domestic Council
and took over from Vice President Agnew the responsibility for
communication and liaison with governors, mayors and county
officials. The reaction to the latter change among Republican governors who visited the President the other day provided an inter-

esting index to the Vice President's standing with them and at the White House. They welcomed the change, saying that at long last they have in Kenneth Cole a White House friend and contact who is where the action is.

February 24, 1973

Ken Cole survived the fall and departure of Ehrlichman, but he soon followed Peter Flanigan from the West Wing to the EOB. Cole in early 1974 replaced former Defense Secretary Melvin Laird, who had briefly replaced Ehrlichman, as the assistant for domestic affairs and returned to the West Wing, in Ehrlichman's and Laird's former office. Dwight Chapin, indicted for perjury, pleaded not guilty and prepared for trial in March of 1974.

Cleaning the Cleaners

Between mid-November and mid-February, when the fourth Nixon message on protection of the environment and the legislative proposals that accompanied it were worked out and sent to Congress, the President didn't give much of his time to discussion of the subject with the White House department and agency officials who put the package together for him. Other matters occupied him. His Indochina "peace with honor" and his expanding accommodation with Communist China were in the making. He was moving to strengthen his command of the federal bureaucracy and, in the process, reorganizing his own White House bureaucracy. He was drawing the lines of battle with Congress over the extent and uses of executive power. With his new budget he was preparing a broad and explosive challenge to the proposition, which had been reflected in dominant American thought and practice since the 1930s, that state and local authority cannot be trusted and only federal authority can be trusted to recognize and meet the nation's social needs. There should have been no wonder, then, that the department and agency officials who did the stoop labor on the environmental message and legislation saw little or nothing of him. He seemed to some of them to be less interested in the business than he professed to be when he spoke in the message and in an introductory radio speech of his scorn for hand-wringing preachers of ecological doom and of his confidence that the American people have "the capacity and character" necessary to "meet our natural resources challenges" and stand with him upon "a sensible middle ground between the Cassandras and the Pollyannas."

A group of conservationists who conferred with Russell E. Train, chairman of the Council on Environmental Quality, after the message was released got an impression that he and others involved in drafting the 1973 program had missed the firm White House direction that they received in 1971 and 1972. Train and his council colleagues met only once with the President, in early January, before the message and the legislation were in final shape and then Mr. Nixon expressed specific interest in only one aspect of the program, the development of a national land-use policy to be implemented by state and local governments with federal support and coordination. Organizational and personnel changes at the White House contributed to a feeling in the concerned departments and agencies that nobody was really in charge of the preparatory operation. John D. Ehrlichman, the assistant for domestic affairs, who in past years had been very definitely in charge, had withdrawn from current routine to concentrate upon what he called more profound issues and problems that the President wanted him to anticipate and think about. Ehrlichman's successor as director of the Domestic Council, Kenneth Cole, appeared to leave the White House role in the formative phase to Richard Fairbanks, a young (aged 32) lawyer who is the assistant director responsible for natural resource affairs, and to William Morrill, an assistant director of the Office of Management and Budget. Secretary of Agriculture Earl Butz, who had been designated by the President to be his counsellor in overall charge of natural resources policy, had barely begun to function in that capacity and took little part in developing the 1973 program. Such department and agency heads as Chairman Train, Administrator William D. Ruckelshaus of the Environmental Protection Agency, and Interior Secretary Rogers Morton might guess that major and disputed points were referred by Fairbanks and Morrill to their superiors and perhaps to the President, but they were not told that this was done. The result was a sense, at the working levels outside the White House, that the President in his search for efficiency and effective command had somehow withdrawn from the very command that he sought to exercise through others and was letting issues of great importance be settled well down in the bureaucracy, by the processes of compromise and trade-off that he says he deplores.

The odd thing is that this was in fact a considerable misapprehension. Mr. Nixon rode closer herd on the preparatory processes than he let anyone beyond his immediate staff know. The decision to drag the issue of farm supports and policy into the environmental message and to make it the vehicle for announcing his proposal to abandon direct agricultural subsidies within the next few years was his alone. Matters that turned out to be in dispute between interested agencies and officials, and some on which Fairbanks simply wanted presidential guidance, were regularly bucked to Kenneth Cole and, on occasion, by Cole to Mr. Nixon. One such was the proposal, new in this year's program, to set forth federal standards for drinking water and authorize citizens to sue their local authorities in federal courts if their water didn't meet the requirements. Another was the proposal to authorize direct federal regulation of the disposal of extremely hazardous industrial wastes instead of leaving the whole responsibility to states and localities. Whether the administration should ask for broader authority than it had previously requested to require advance planning of power plant sites and tighter federal coordination of state supervision of the planning was put up to the President and he decided in favor of a strengthened proposal. These were touchy questions, of more concern to the President than they might appear to be to the casual citizen, because of Mr. Nixon's prior insistence to the departments and agencies and in his message that the federal government "must not displace state and local initiative" and that he expects "state and local governments—along with the private sector—to play the central role" in environmental control.

The issue in fiercest dispute within and between the agencies and departments, and the one that provided the clearest indicator of the administration's purpose and courage, was the regulation of surface mining. Nothing in the entire preliminary phase was more puzzling to the working-level advocates and opponents of strong federal control than the impression in which they were left that the President and his principal domestic adviser, John Ehrlichman, kept themselves remote from this controversy as well as from others and allowed it to be resolved in the middle bureaucracy. It in fact was one of the several issues that went to Cole and ultimately to the President for final decision. Ehrlichman stayed out of the direct line of fire, but he kept in touch with the controversy as it developed. His principal assignment at the moment is the preparation of a major policy message dealing with the whole problem of energy supply and strip-mined coal, among other sources, and he is setting up a special White House staff apart from Cole's Domestic Council staff to exercise presidential supervision in this area. The central point at issue on strip mining was whether and how the administration should strengthen the weak regulatory bill that it sent up and Congress ignored last year. The bill finally approved by the President and sent to Congress still leaves the initial and primary responsibility for regulation to the states. It still gives them two years to come up with laws and regulations that meet federal standards and, in the revised version, allows strip miners a third year in which to satisfy the state requirements. Real enforcement, whether by the states or by the federal government if the states fail to impose adequate regulation, would in effect be deferred a full five years after enactment of the federal law. In these respects the submitted legislation represented a defeat for the chief advocates of strong regulation, Train at the Council for Environmental Quality and Ruckelshaus at EPA. Judged by these factors alone, the strip-mining bill may be said to show that the President's environmental cleaners were taken to the cleaners in the review process. But that isn't the whole story. The President approved proposals that the federal standards the states and eventually the strip miners have to meet be spelled out early and explicitly, as they were not in his past legislation, and that the standards themselves be high enough to curb though by no means to end the outrage that surface mining works upon the land. Here, as in other aspects of the Nixon approach to environmental protection, the fair judgment has to be that the President proposes a lot less than is needed; a lot more than any of his predecessors have proposed; and a lot more, too, than anyone would have expected Richard Nixon to undertake.

March 3, 1973

———

The critical oil and other energy shortages that developed in late 1973 and early 1974 enabled Mr. Nixon to retreat all along the environmental line from the positions noted in this report.

Two Loners

A new book is out with a fascinating account, the best that I've seen, of the way in which Richard Nixon and Henry Kissinger have worked together to alter the shape and course of United States foreign policy and, as the President justly said in China last year, to "change the world." The book is *The Retreat of American Power* (Doubleday; $8.95). Its author is Henry Brandon, an associate editor and for 23 years the chief Washington correspondent of the London *Sunday Times*. Its thesis is that the President and Kissinger between them have devised and the President has successfully and prudently conducted "an orderly retreat from obsolete global commitments to safer and more solid positions . . . without serious adverse consequences on world security."

In order to sustain the thesis, Brandon has to take the so-called Nixon Doctrine at face value and with total seriousness. He must and does excuse the ambiguities and contradictions in which Mr. Nixon has expressed his doctrine ever since he first enunciated it on the island of Guam in 1969, in a rambling and confusing dissertation to reporters that to this day has not been put on the public record, on the ground that the obfuscation has been necessary in order "to lead the retreat of American power in a responsible way, fast enough to maintain support at home and slow enough not to lose confidence abroad or to tempt the enemy into wrong assumptions." Brandon also must and does accept at face value the President's familiar claim that he has had to frame and apply his policy of readjustment abroad in such a way as to withstand and beat back a "wave of new isolationism" at home. "What we had to do first," Mr. Nixon told Brandon and a visiting London editor in February 1970, "was to make it plain to the American people that in fact we cannot opt out of the world, and second, to seek their support in continuing a policy even though it is a policy of revised involvement." I doubt that the President has ever really believed that he had to convince significant numbers of Americans that "we cannot opt out of the world," and a less considerate writer than the sensitive and gracious Henry Brandon might call Mr. Nixon's "policy of revised involvement" a policy of continuing commitment on the cheap. These are minor carpings. With them vented, I turn from the major proposition of an admirable book to its perceptive account and analysis of the relationship between the President and Henry Kissinger.

Brandon knew and admired Kissinger and knew and did not admire Richard Nixon long before the President won his second nomination at Miami Beach in 1968. In a telephone conversation after that occurrence, Brandon recalls, "Kissinger not only confirmed all my fears and misgivings, but reinforced them in no uncertain terms. He shared my mistrust of the man and his character." Kissinger, who had been Governor Nelson Rockefeller's foreign affairs adviser since the 1950s and had assisted his efforts to do Nixon out of the Republican nominations in 1960 and 1968, told Brandon that he "profoundly distrusted" Nixon and "served Rockefeller to keep Nixon out." Kissinger said he thought and feared that Nixon lacked principle, lacked the inner security and confidence a leader needs, and was "frozen" in a "cold-war outlook" that could induce him to take "undue risks" in a time of "waning military preeminence." Much later, Kissinger told Brandon that "he remained distrustful until he actually began to work for the President." Brandon's detailed account of how Nixon and

Kissinger got together after the election, partly at the urging of and upon the recommendation of others, comes to this: it took Professor Henry Kissinger of Harvard—"a poor German refugee" and "a German-born Jew"—two meetings and five days to overcome his distrust sufficiently to agree to be Nixon's assistant for national security affairs and enter upon a relationship that "grew into something unprecedented in American history." Kissinger became "the President's de facto Secretary of State" and "his loyal, most personal, most dedicated servant rather than, as one cynical comment put it, his Rasputin."

How did this come about? One of Brandon's several answers is that Nixon knew in 1968, from Kissinger's writings, that he and Kissinger "held a shared view about how the United States should deal with the Russians and Chinese—not as ideological powers, but on the basis of a mutual interest with which no middle power should be allowed to interfere." Other shared views and characteristics—dislike of the State Department, a disdain for bureaucracy, and "a conspiratorial mind, a penchant for secret diplomacy and the *coup de théâtre*"—drew them to each other. Brandon gets closest to the inward answers, answers that Kissinger has said nobody except himself and the President will ever really get at, in two analytic passages.

"Kissinger," Brandon writes, "has the rare gift of being a conceptual thinker, a quality which separates the intellectual from the politician and which made Kissinger a particularly valuable aide, for he was able to give the President's policy instincts intellectual content. The President is not a profound thinker, but he can ask profound questions, and Kissinger's ability to give him the answers, to explain to the President where he might find himself half a dozen moves from where he stood, gave Mr. Nixon the kind of intellectual sense of security he needed."

Brandon observes that "their relationship grew in intimacy and yet retained a formality which neither ever dropped." Then he writes: "They are also both loners, and in a theatrical sense, tragic figures who have achieved more than they ever expected, and yet lack the contentment and happiness it ought to bring. Neither can come close to anyone for fear of being unable to meet the demands of friendship or intimacy. They hold enormous power in their hands, but they remain in isolation. Both suffer from insecurities and feel the need of reassurance, but both have gained confidence from the use of power. Kissinger has been accused of displaying an arrogance of power, but if anything his fault is an arrogance of intellect which makes him believe that he can control and manage reality. This also leads him, if the facts do not vindicate his theories, to believe that the facts are wrong. His insecurities also develop from a sense of being disliked, of being surrounded by enemies, or of losing support among those he cares about, and from attacks in newspapers which tend to upset him as much as they do other public personalities. His most obvious insecurities, however, are his total dependence on getting his ideas accepted and his need for protection from his adversaries, of which he has as many as most eminences grises did in history."

Brandon suggests that Kissinger's steadfast loyalty during the Cambodia "incursion" in 1970 sealed his and Nixon's friendship. Although he deplored the President's bellicose announcement of the action, Kissinger "stood like a rock" with Nixon against the protests that erupted nationally and within the White House. Secretaries Rogers and Laird "enraged the President" by intimating their doubts to the press and thereafter "he had reservations about both of them."

Brandon had to close out his book for the printers before ups and downs in the final Vietnam negotiations and some White House leaks fostered an impression of differences between the President and Kissinger and of sharper differences between Kissinger and certain other assistants, notably (though Brandon doesn't name them) John D. Ehrlichman and H. R. Haldeman. Brandon, however, sensed the makings of friction before most other outsiders did. He writes that Kissinger "was careful to ensure that the President would harvest the ultimate credit for all foreign policy achievements, but the spectacular visibility and fulsome credit he was given by the media after a time began to grate on the President. Some men of the President's inner circle resented the massive publicity even more than Mr. Nixon." Former Commerce Secretary Peter G. Peterson is quoted: "Henry's relation with the White House staff is as intimate as was that between Caesar and Brutus."

In a remark that foreshadowed his famous and misguided burst of vainglory in an interview last November with Italian journalist Oriana Fallaci, Kissinger once said to Brandon: "Often I don't know whether I am the actor or the director." He takes care nowadays to behave and talk as if he knows that Richard Nixon is the director.

Although Brandon doesn't try to guess at how long Kissinger will remain at the Nixon White House, he knows from continuing acquaintance that the question of whether and when to leave is never far from Kissinger's thoughts. "Publishers have offered him contracts in six figures," Brandon writes, "and yet he is worried about the future, less for its financial aspects than what kind of job he should seek and what that loss of power may do to him psychologically."

March 10, 1973

———

I erred in saying the President's Guam statement of the Nixon Doctrine was not on the public record. It was inserted, without announcement, in the 1969 volume of *Public Papers of the President*.

VIII

"I Run the Campaign"

During a televised interview on January 4, 1971, after saying that the rebroadcast on the night before the 1970 congressional elections of the crudest of his several crude attacks on crude dissenters was a mistake that wouldn't have happened if he had been "running the campaign," President Nixon added: "Incidentally, when I am the candidate, I run the campaign."

Getting Mr. Nixon, his chief assistants and his White House spokesmen to acknowledge that he ran his 1972 campaign in the inclusive sense that he indicated with his 1971 remark has been a vain endeavor since he announced his candidacy for renomination and reelection early last year. The temptation to attribute the difficulty of demonstrating that the President followed his own maxim in 1972 to the Watergate bugging case and the continuing disclosures of the campaign crookery that it set off is almost irresistible. But the temptation has to be resisted in the interest

of truth, the truth being that Mr. Nixon created an elaborate structure of concealment months before the scandals began to break.

The structures that hid his management of the campaign were
his Committee for the Re-election of the President and its affiliated
finance committee. It may be, of course, that he anticipated at
least some of the chicanery that occurred and the necessity to
insulate himself from it. That is supposition, however, and a
reasonable assumption is that the purpose evident at the time the
committees were organized, along with a cooperating and covert
campaign apparatus within the White House establishment, was
the main and sufficient purpose. It was to enable Mr. Nixon to
run as a President occupied with the business of the presidency,
leaving the practical politics of the operation to the politicians and
technicians who headed and staffed the committees and, behind
the scenes, the aforementioned White House apparatus. Foresight
may have figured, as has been suggested. But even so canny and
experienced a politician as Richard Nixon can hardly have foreseen that the concealing structures would finally conceal, or importantly help to conceal, any connection that he may have had
with activities that have caused the reelection committee to be
fined $8000, confronted seven of its employees and retainers with
criminal charges and prospective prison sentences, and tarred one
of the President's brothers, one of his closest assistants, and at
least one of his former Cabinet officers with complicity in rascalities ranging from probably illegal and certainly improper solicitation and disbursement of political contributions to use of those
funds for spying upon and sabotaging the Democratic opposition.

The ultimate irony of the situation is that the concealing mechanisms worked really well only after it became absolutely necessary
for them to work well—which is to say, with the disclosure of behavior that would discredit the President and besmirch his presidency beyond recovery if personal responsibility for any of it was
admitted by him and his spokesmen or provably traced to him. The
pressure of the latest revelations is beginning to tell; *nothing* may
work well enough very much longer; but up to this writing, thanks
in part to the extraordinary loyalty and discretion of the people in
the President's immediate service, it cannot be said that he, personally, has been connected or associated in the slightest degree

with any of the disclosed skullduggery. And that is all that he requires. The reading at the White House is that no critical harm will
be done, that nothing catastrophic to the President and his presidency will develop from the continuing and enlarging scandal, if
only the insulation of the President himself from the sordid business can be sustained and preserved.

The irony just mentioned lies in the circumstance that the President's close and detailed management of his 1972 campaign was
never effectively concealed; yet any responsibility that he may have
for the more sordid aspects of the campaign has been very effectively concealed. The cover for his management was so transparent
that Mr. Nixon cannot have taken it seriously or expected others
to take it seriously. His reelection and finance committees were
headed and principally staffed by men who were placed there, the
chief among them assigned to their campaign jobs by the President himself, because they were known to be his men—wholly
loyal, wholly dedicated to his reelection, men who could be absolutely counted upon never to do anything that they didn't know
or have reason to suppose he'd want them to do. It's a familiar
roster, but worth recounting in this context.

The reelection committee's first director was the President's
former law partner, the manager of his 1968 campaign and his
first attorney general, John Mitchell. Its second and last director
was Clark MacGregor, who was transferred from the White House
staff to replace Mitchell when he resigned—not because, some at
the White House said, of possible involvement in the Watergate
scandal, but because the President and his top domestic assistants,
H. R. Haldeman and John Ehrlichman, wanted to assert and maintain closer control of the committee than they could with so great
and independent a Nixon grandee as John Mitchell at its head.
One of Haldeman's White House protégés, Jeb S. Magruder, and
Fred Malek, the President's chief personnel recruiter, were the
committee's deputy directors. The head of the finance committee,
the campaign's Mister Money, was and still is former Commerce
Secretary Maurice Stans. One of Stans' assistants was the President's brother, Edward Nixon, who according to sworn testimony
shared and furthered Stans' passion for cash contributions in large
amounts. If the President wanted to know and didn't know all there

was to know about this aspect of the committee and campaign operation, all he had to do was ask his brother. So many White House assistants turned up on the two committee staffs and Mitchell, MacGregor and Stans spent so much of their time at the White House, in consultation with the President and his assistants, Haldeman and Ehrlichman, that the projected image of the committees as independent entities became a standing joke among White House and political reporters. Before and after the President's renomination, Press Secretary Ronald Ziegler regularly referred questions about Mr. Nixon's political doings and plans to his counterpart, also a White House transfer, at the reelection committee. In short the reelection and finance committees were and still are, in their remarkably prolonged post-election afterlife, extensions and adjuncts of the Nixon White House, at the disposal and command, sometimes direct and sometimes indirect, of the President. He was the candidate and he ran the campaign, as he had said he would.

Now the taint of campaign misbehavior has spread from the committees to the White House. Patrick Gray, the President's nominee to be director of the FBI, has given the Senate Judiciary Committee FBI evidence that Dwight L. Chapin, nominally and until recently the President's appointments secretary and actually one of his principal campaign operatives last year, recruited a young California lawyer and college classmate, Donald Segretti, to direct spying and sabotage aimed at the Democrats. Herbert Kalmbach, a California lawyer who has raised money for Nixon campaigns and represented the President in legal matters, told the FBI that he, at Chapin's direction, paid out between $30,000 and $40,000 of campaign money—Kalmbach didn't keep a record—to Segretti for services unknown to Kalmbach. Chapin was the President's man and, second only to Nixon, Bob Haldeman's man. We are asked to believe that he left their service for a private job (with United Airlines) at his own initiative and solely "for the sake of his family and career." We are asked, too, to believe that the President's and Haldeman's man did what the FBI says Kalmbach said he did without the knowledge or authority of either the President or Haldeman.

We have it from both Patrick Gray and John Ehrlichman that Bob Haldeman was not among the 14 White House assistants questioned by the FBI in connection with the Watergate affair. Who's surprised? Not I. Ehrlichman was one of the 14. He says he wasn't asked what if anything he might know about the Watergate or related matters; only ·about two defendants in that case, Howard Hunt and Gordon Liddy, who once worked for him at the White House. Ehrlichman said he didn't know anything worth telling. Who believes that? Not I. The President's young staff counsel, John Wesley Dean III, is "invited" to testify for the Senate Judiciary Committee on Gray's confirmation, and the President is on record personally and in a formal statement with his absolute refusal, on the traditional grounds of executive privilege, to let him do it. The interesting thing about John Dean is not that, as the President says, he established by investigation at the White House that nobody employed there when the Watergate case broke last summer knew anything about it or had anything to do with it. The interesting thing, adroitly obscured by the President and his senior assistants, is that Dean's primary assignment since last summer has been to follow, for the President, all of the sundry official investigations of all aspects of the manifold campaign scandals. He is bound to know more than the press and public, not to mention Congress, are ever likely to know about them and about what the President knows about them.

March 24, 1973

———

Nothing that I have written about the Nixon presidency was more deeply resented at the White House than my resurrection of his 1971 statement that "I run the campaign." He shortly, on April 30, was to take pains to explain how and why he didn't (he says) in 1972.

Jerks and Jitters

Three press conferences within six weeks were not unprecedented for Mr. Nixon (he held three between June 22 and July 27 last year). But the frequency was unusual and he seemed to enjoy the evident surprise of reporters when he suddenly turned up at the microphones and before the cameras in the White House press room on March 15. The conveyed impression, however, was that the surprise was the only thing about this third appearance since January 31 that he enjoyed. A look of strain and weariness came through to some of us in the room and, viewers told me later, from the filmed snatches shown on television. The President's voice shook and wavered. When I checked a transcript of the conference against a tape recording, I wrote "tremor" beside ten passages. All of the tremors occurred when the President was dealing with two subjects, the difficulty of making his peace with honor stick in Indochina and his conflict with the Senate over its inquiries into scandals arising from the conduct of his 1972 reelection campaign. His answers and events at the White House during the next few days indicated that he was troubled by other matters, notably the persistent and inflationary rise of food prices. But Vietnam and the scandals seemed to be the problems that bothered the President most and contributed most to the impression that this, for him, was a jerky and jittery time.

The ostensible purpose of the press conference was to announce the President's selection of David K. E. Bruce, aged 75 and a millionaire and one of the country's distinguished diplomats, to head up the US liaison office, actually an embassy but not called that, to be opened on or around May 1 in Peking. Mr. Nixon said he "thought it was very important to appoint a man of great stature to this position," and his announcement constituted an invitation to the Chinese Communists to choose a figure of equal distinction to head their mission in Washington. It was the conclusive signal, if any were needed, that the long US relation with and support of Chiang Kai-Shek's Republic of China on Taiwan is a fading factor, not to be allowed to impede accommodation with Communist China.

With that out of the way, the questions soon brought the President to his evident and primary reason for appearing that day. It was to warn the North Vietnamese government that he is prepared to resume and is capable of resuming military action against North Vietnam if Hanoi continues to send war equipment into South Vietnam on a scale that the President believes to be "a violation of the cease-fire . . . and the peace agreement." There was a palpable chill in the press room when, after remarking that the North Vietnamese and "other interested parties" (meaning Moscow and Peking) had been told "of our concern about this infiltration," the President said: ". . . I would only suggest that based on my actions over the past four years, that the North Vietnamese should not lightly disregard such expressions of concern." He was deliberately recalling his invasion of Cambodia, his bombardment and mining of North Vietnam in May of 1972, the fierce bombardment in December, all after warnings that he would do whatever he thought necessary to prevent or punish what he considered to be unacceptable North Vietnamese behavior. Did he mean it this time? I think he did, although questions would arise in the next few days about his authority to act on his own, once the withdrawal of American military forces from South Vietnam was completed as agreed on March 28. The last time the President was called upon to justify military action taken upon his sole authority as Commander-in-Chief, he said he had the constitutional power and duty to protect American forces in combat situations. After March 28 there would be none to protect in South Vietnam. But I suspect that Mr. Nixon, despite the furies certain to be aroused in Congress and in the country, would again prove himself capable of taking the kind of retaliatory action he has taken before if he thought it necessary. In such an event, he would be likely to note in his customarily bland and imperious way that he still had air and naval forces to protect in Thailand and off the shores of Indochina. His party's leader in the Senate, Hugh Scott of Pennsylvania, one of many co-sponsors of a resolution that would impose presently nonexistent limits upon the President's power of independent military action, indicated at the White House on March 20 that he, too, thinks Mr. Nixon has the authority and the will to do what he threatened to do on the 15th. Once he had sounded off, the President's spokesmen tried to diminish the heat of his warning. But any conclusion from this that it was all a bluff would be a misreading of Richard Nixon.

The President's responses and nonresponses to questions arising from the campaign scandals and inquiries told more about him as a person, it seemed to me, than anything else I recall his saying in a long while. Consider, for example, the way he dealt with the troubles besetting his nomination of his loyal servant and political supporter, L. Patrick Gray, to be director of the FBI. The gut of it is that Mr. Nixon dumped Pat Gray. The President neglected several opportunities to say that he still supported the nomination as strongly as he had said he did on March 2. He rebuked Gray for offering raw FBI files to any and all members of the Senate Judiciary Committee and, with a minimal pretense of compassion ("I understand why Mr. Gray did, his hearing was involved"), said in the coldest possible tone that "the practice of the FBI furnishing 'raw files' to full committees must stop with this particular one." The fact that this and a good deal else in the way of voluntary disclosure stopped forthwith became apparent when Gray, at resumed hearings on his nomination, said he had been ordered to refuse further answers to specific questions about the FBI's investigation of the Watergate bugging and the White House staff's oversight of that investigation.

A special committee headed by Senator Sam J. Ervin of North Carolina is preparing to investigate the Watergate and other campaign irregularities and the prospect was very much on the President's mind. Speaking of the Ervin committee, Mr. Nixon said "I do not intend to raise questions about its conduct" and proceeded to raise several questions. His staff counsel and his chief overseer of all the investigations, John Wesley Dean III, would not be allowed to testify in person but he would accept written questions and provide all requested information "provided it is pertinent to the investigation." *If* the investigation proved to be a "bipartisan" look into "both election campaigns," *if* Senator Ervin fulfilled what the President took to be his promises that he "will accept no hearsay; that he will not tolerate any guilt by innuendo; that he will not tolerate any guilt by association"—then, the President indicated, the committee would have all the cooperation and information it wanted from the administration and the White House. Senator Ervin had yet to say, as he did on television the following Sunday, that he'd ask the Senate to send its sergeant-at-arms to arrest Dean or any other White House assistant who refused to testify in person. Mr. Nixon appeared to anticipate such a confrontation when he invited a Supreme Court test of the tradition of executive privilege upon which he relied.

One of the tremors in Mr. Nixon's voice came with his reference to "hearsay . . . guilt by innuendo . . . guilt by association." Richard Nixon had indulged freely in those instruments of political combat when he ran for his House and Senate seats and when he was a congressman, senator and Vice President. It may be doubted, however, that recollection of past sins accounted for the show of emotion. A current and more likely reason was that "guilt by innuendo" and "guilt by association" are the only forms of guilt in the unsavory campaign doings of last year that can presently the charged to Mr. Nixon. In this dark light, two of his responses at the March 15 press conference were especially interesting.

When he was asked whether he knew at the time that his former appointments secretary and close assistant, Dwight Chapin, had

been involved in a documented arrangement to spy upon and
sabotage the 1972 Democratic primary campaigns, the President
professed to welcome "an opportunity to . . . answer that question" and then didn't answer it. He launched instead into his dissertation upon the proper conduct of Senator Ervin's investigation.
Another question dealt with his Committee for the Re-election of
the President and, by implication, with the Watergate and campaign funds scandal that marred its performance. "Where," a
reporter asked, "do you feel your responsibility for the Committee
to Reelect the President [*sic*] begins and ends?" It was a way of
asking whether the President acknowledged any responsibility for
the reelection and affiliated finance committees' operations under
former Attorney General John Mitchell, former Commerce Secretary Maurice Stans, and the many former White House employees
who worked with them during the campaign. Mr. Nixon answered
in part: "Well, the responsibility there, of course, is one that will
be replied to by Mr. Mitchell, Mr. Stans and all of those in due
course." He was saying in effect, as the circumstances compel him
to say, that the responsibility neither begins nor ends with him.

March 31, 1973

X

Sunshine Summitry

San Clemente

At the end of the occasion that the press is calling the San Clemente Summit, President Nixon refrained from saying what he said about President Thieu of South Vietnam after their last meeting in Saigon on July 30, 1969. Talking to reporters on his plane during his flight from Saigon to Bangkok and admonishing them not to put his words between quotation marks, Mr. Nixon said then that Nguyen Van Thieu was probably one of the four or five best political leaders in the world. This time Mr. Nixon contented himself with saying in effect that he expects the people of South Vietnam to keep their president in office when and if the "genuinely free and democratic general elections" promised in the Vietnam peace agreement are ever held. Mr. Nixon could not have stated his expectation in so many words without violating the undertaking in the Vietnam agreement that "the United States will not . . . intervene in the internal affairs of South Vietnam." He got the message across by saying, in brief and graceful farewell remarks on the sunny lawn of his California home, that he and President

Thieu had been having "very constructive talks with regard to how we shall work together in the years ahead" and telling the smiling little man at his side that "we wish you well as you go on to Washington and as you return to your own country."

Some of the heavy thinkers in the Nixon press party quickly fell to guessing that Thieu got a good deal less from this meeting than he hoped to get, particularly in the way of an explicit pledge to him and threat to the Hanoi Communists that the US will again come to the military defense of South Vietnam if it is again attacked from North Vietnam or by the North Vietnamese forces remaining in South Vietnam. All I know about that at this writing is that President Thieu looked a lot happier when he parted from President Nixon in San Clemente than he did at the close of their meeting on Midway Island in June 1969. Then, just after being told that the withdrawal of American ground forces from Vietnam was about to begin, Thieu seemed to me to be shaken and forlorn. Here in San Clemente, on the afternoon of his second and final day with Mr. Nixon, President Thieu had the look of a pleased and confident guest who had heard from his host what he expected to hear and wasn't disappointed by it. When he and Mr. Nixon walked together from the President's home to the helicopter pad beside the office quarters at the Western White House, Thieu's step was positively jaunty. He hopped aboard a waiting presidential chopper and turned at the door for a last wave to the cameras as if he owned the vehicle.

It was a meeting that Thieu has been yearning for and nudging Mr. Nixon toward ever since the Midway encounter. "We may agree together to meet again," Thieu said rather wistfully at Midway. He said in Saigon, when Mr. Nixon paused there on his 1969 swing around the world, that at Midway the two of them had "agreed to meet at regular intervals." At San Clemente, after an interval of nearly four years, the ceremonial honors and entertainments were considerably short of what they would have been if President Nixon had chosen to receive his friend and ally at the White House in Washington with the full panoply of a "state visit" instead of the "official visit" that this one turned out to be. But there were compensations, not the least for Mr. Nixon being that he could stay in California and confer upon Vice

President Agnew the doubtful privilege of playing host to Thieu in Washington under the eyes of a Congress that was restive about the continuing American bombardment in Cambodia and the growing difficulty of detecting with much certainty either the peace or the honor in the proclaimed peace with honor.

One of the compensations for all concerned, including a large press party that saw very little of the event and learned less about the closed discussions, was simply that Southern California in the spring, when the weather is as kind as it was to Presidents Nixon and Thieu, is a wonderful place for friends to meet and display their friendship. In his only public appearances with Thieu, at the beginning and end of the meeting, Mr. Nixon seemed to be enjoying the affair as much as his visitor was. I got a notion, watching the easy way in which he handled himself and his guest, that he welcomed the occasion partly because it took his mind and (he must have hoped) the public mind off the Watergate and associated campaign scandals and the deepening embroilment with the Senate that they were driving him into.

The principals apart, there were some witnessed and memorable vignettes. Thieu had publicly derided and denounced Henry Kissinger for negotiating and accepting in October an agreement with the North Vietnamese that "would mean abandoning South Vietnam" and had thanked Mr. Nixon for rejecting it and demanding the revisions that resulted in the agreement of January 23. Kissinger had said that Thieu would accept any agreement that suited the United States because "he has to." How, then, would they greet each other in San Clemente? They greeted each other with smiles and a seemingly warm handshake. When Thieu in his arrival speech remarked with wry satisfaction that the US has had to keep 300,000 troops in Western Europe while withdrawing its ground forces from South Vietnam, Kissinger grinned and chortled as if he wished that he had made the crack. Before the two Presidents appeared to speak their farewells, the senior officials with Thieu and the senior American officials lined up in separate groups on the Nixon lawn. The Vietnamese stood in placid quiet. Kissinger regaled the Americans with what they, as judged by their overheard laughter, took to be uproarious jokes. He noted that Secretary of

State Rogers had the place of honor at the head of the American line and growled, "He's hard enough to deal with as it is." Kissinger got another big laugh when he said to Rogers, "If you call me 'Doctor,' I'll call you 'Honorable.' " The advent of the Presidents, 30 minutes behind schedule, put a merciful end to this exercise in White House humor.

The only substantial resemblance between the San Clemente Summit and Mr. Nixon's Peking and Moscow Summits was that a joint communiqué was issued at the close of this one too. My impression is that it could have been written without benefit of a meeting, but there is evidence that it actually was composed or at least completed here in San Clemente. Press Secretary Ronald Ziegler told reporters on the second morning that they would have the communiqué "as soon as we get it finished" and it was delivered to the press an hour after Ziegler had said it would be. On the assumption that readers will have been surfeited with learned interpretations of the document by the time this is read, I briefly summarize what I find to be the most interesting points in it and suggested by it.

The predictable warning to the North Vietnamese and Vietcong Communists that the US will renew military action in Vietnam if the cease-fire is violated by them more seriously than it has been to date is noticeably milder than Mr. Nixon's previous warnings to the same effect were. There is, naturally and expectably, only the most oblique recognition of the fact that Thieu's government and armed forces have been violating the agreement and breaking the cease-fire. But the recognition is there and it suggests that President Nixon told President Thieu that improved behavior is expected from him as well as from his enemies. A reference to Mr. Nixon's "great interest" in the abortive Paris negotiations between the Thieu government and the Communist Provisional Government of South Vietnam, aimed with mutual and obvious lack of enthusiasm at arranging the promised general elections in South Vietnam, suggests that Thieu was told that his behavior in this respect could also stand some improvement. The major emphasis of the communiqué, however, is upon "the enduring relationship of friendship which exists between the government of the Republic of Vietnam and the United States." Mr. Nixon had

decided before the meeting to keep US economic aid to South
Vietnam at an annual level of around $600 million and, Congress
willing, to sustain military assistance at or near the level of $1.6
billion projected in his 1974 budget. If things settle down in South
Vietnam and the rest of Indochina, the military figure may be
reduced. With the communiqué and the meeting in San Clemente,
Mr. Nixon is telling us that the American involvement in Indochina is going to last and telling President Thieu that he can count
on his friend in the White House to make it last, at any necessary
cost.

April 14, 1973

Kissinger thought it was very wrong of me to quote and, he said,
misquote persiflage that was overheard over a loudspeaker system
that he and his companions didn't know was on. He was right. I
apologize.

XI

Trade-offs for Trade

The President postponed to the very last any close and active participation in the preparation of the foreign trade message and legislation that he sent to Congress on April 10. He left to his advisers, and there were plenty of them, the spadework on the message, his voluminous Trade Reform Act of 1973, and supporting proposals to remove antitrust restrictions on collaborating bidders for foreign business and to retain, while slightly reducing, the tax breaks given American companies that invest in and operate foreign subsidiaries. His designated formulators and kibitzers included George Shultz, acting in his dual capacities as secretary of the Treasury and assistant to the President in charge of overall economic policy; Peter Flanigan, the executive director of the President's Council on International Economic Policy; John D. Ehrlichman, the assistant for domestic affairs; Herbert Stein, chairman of the Council of Economic Advisers; Chairman Arthur Burns of the Federal Reserve Board; and William Pearce, deputy special representative for foreign trade negotiation. They had for guidance the President's many statements of foreign trade policy, beginning with his pledge to work for "an open world" in his 1969 inaugural address and, in subsequent actions and expressions over the next four years, weighted toward a fundamentally protectionist position. They assumed that Mr. Nixon would want the legislation and especially the message, in which he would be setting forth his own philosophy and trying to satisfy both the extreme protectionists and the advocates of what used to be and no longer is called "free trade," weighted in the same direction.

When Mr. Nixon finally gave personal attention to the message, in the last days and hours before it was submitted to Congress and published, his advisers and the White House writers who had put an initial draft together for him got an interesting surprise. The President removed many references to his past moves to protect American textile, steel, oil and other interests in competition with foreign producers and strengthened the emphasis upon his professed desire for "a more open and equitable world trading system" and upon his view that "we must resist the impulse to turn inward." A pronounced protectionist tone remained, but the net effect of the President's changes was to place the philosophical thrust on what he and his assistants prefer to style "open trade" and "balanced trade" rather than "free trade" that never has been and probably never can be genuinely and wholly "free."

One of Mr. Nixon's interventions was a crashing bust. He had his writers extract from the message and condense a passage that he prerecorded for national television. Mr. Nixon usually puts enough substance into such blurbs to give them at least a semblance of news and enable the networks to carry them without seeming to kowtow in utter abjection to the presidential will. The 63 words he taped in 35 seconds were all blurb and no substance ("The trade bill . . . can mean more jobs and better jobs for American workmen . . . help American consumers . . . help us expand our trade . . . reduce international tensions.") and the news executives of all three television networks rebelled. The foreign trade blurb got some scattered radio use but the filmed version didn't appear on any of the evening news shows at which it was aimed.

Secretary Shultz and Peter Flanigan got more notice and publicity with a White House briefing for the media than the President

did. In one of their exchanges between themselves and with reporters, they also dramatized the delicate play of contending forces
that will determine the fate of the Nixon proposals in Congress.
A reporter set off the exchange when he asked Shultz whether he
would agree that the President was seeking "new and unprecedented authorities" to determine and administer national trade
policy. Inasmuch as Mr. Nixon had said in his message that he
was asking Congress "to delegate significant new negotiating authorities to the executive branch," Shultz and Flanigan should have
had no difficulty in answering the question. But they did. When
Shultz agreed with the reporter that "the President would be given
authority that he had not been given before," Peter Flanigan was
seen to flinch. Obviously with congressional resistance to any increase in the President's power in mind, Flanigan stepped to the
microphones and said he wouldn't dream of contradicting Secretary
Shultz. Then he did, arguing that speaking of "new and unprecedented authorities" is "overstating the case" and that "while these
are expansions of existing authority, they aren't radically new departures from past practice." Shultz took the contradiction in pen-
sive silence, with the look of a man who has acknowledged the
truth and recognizes a necessary and tactical correction when he
hears it.

Mr. Nixon's statement and definition of the new authorities he
was seeking were perfect examples of the trade-offs for trade that
studded his message and legislation. For instance, he requested authority limited only in time (five years) to "eliminate, reduce or
increase customs duties" in the course of conducting the kind of
trade negotiations that are coming up next fall on a worldwide
scale. As a gesture toward the many senators and congressmen
who will balk at so broad a grant of unrestricted presidential
power, he invited Congress "to set up whatever mechanism it
deems best for closer consultation and cooperation" with him while
such negotiations are going on. He moderated his request for
broadened power to impose, remove or change such nontariff bar-
riers as quantitative quotas for imports in return for or retaliation
against similar trade actions by other governments with an offer of
limited though substantial congressional oversight. He would give
interested congressional committees 90 days notice of intended

nontariff changes and, after they were agreed and decided upon, another 90 days in which either the House or Senate could veto any change by majority vote. As it is now Congress must amend existing law before negotiated agreements on nontariff changes can take effect.

Similar trade-offs were proposed in such sensitive areas as American investment in foreign enterprises and the taxation of profits earned abroad by American subsidiaries. A protectionist bill sponsored by Senator Vance Hartke of Indiana would abolish the present deferral of US taxes upon the profits of American subsidiaries until the money is brought home and also end the deduction of taxes paid by subsidiaries to foreign governments from the taxable income of the owning American companies. Aware though he is of formidable support for the Hartke proposals, Mr. Nixon argued that the present policy of encouraging American investment and production abroad "is still fundamentally sound" and offered only modest concessions to the industrialists and labor leaders who regard the consequences as threats to American producers and workers. The President would subject the profits of American subsidiaries to immediate US taxation only if more than 25 percent of their output is exported for sale in US markets or if they have been demonstrably established in order to escape US taxes and take advantage of excessive foreign tax inducements.

The President sought to attract the support of organized labor for his proposals with recommendations that he at once be given more flexible power to compensate workers displaced from jobs as a result of foreign competition in home markets and to impose either higher tariffs or quotas upon imports that clearly disrupt the home market. In essence, a simple declaration without the elaborate supporting proof now required that competitive imports in fact damage home industries or cause loss of home jobs would be sufficient to authorize the imposition of protective restraints. Displaced workers would (he promised) find it easier to apply for and get unemployment compensation, qualify for federally financed retraining for other jobs, and even get federal money to pay the expenses of moving from one job to another. In the main, however, the President proposed to shift from arrangements designed only for workers displaced by foreign competition to generalized arrangements that would assist and protect workers who lose jobs for any reason. He argued, for example, that his forthcoming "comprehensive pension reform legislation," requiring that a worker's pension rights be transferrable from one job and employer to another, would benefit the victims of foreign competition along with everybody else and should therefore diminish the demand of organized labor for more protective restraints than he is inclined to request or impose.

The message, the legislation and the explanatory White House briefings were parts of an impressive balancing act in behalf of the Nixon vision of "balanced trade." George Shultz, echoing the President's plea for the power and freedom he thinks necessary to deal with the country's trading competitors and adversaries, stated the administration's view with force and clarity when he said: "We must be in a position to drive for more open trade but also drive for trade conditions that are fair for the American working man and for the American businessman." Something for everybody, in short, and certainly something for the American businessman.

April 21, 1973

———

At the close of 1973, I note with morbid interest that the President's request for authority to give the Soviet Union as fair a break as any other country gets in trade with the United States was not mentioned in the preceding pieces. So sane and trite a notion didn't seem worth mention then.

XII

Voice from the Right

It is altogether fitting that this piece about and derived from *The New Majority,* a small book written for the Girard Bank of Philadelphia and published by it for promotional giveaway to some 30,000 customers and friends, should begin with some of the objective reporting that the author advocates in the course of denouncing "advocacy journalism." The frontispiece is a photograph of President Nixon with the author. This and 16 other photographs in the book were taken by Ollie Atkins, who is identified as "the personal photographer to President Nixon." The President appears in 15 of the 17 pictures. The author's introductory note is printed in the form of a facsimile of White House stationery. It is headed "The White House, Washington," and it is signed in longhand and print, "Patrick J. Buchanan, Special Consultant to the President." Buchanan says in the note that "two gentlemen" from the bank called upon him "in late December of 1972, just prior to the Christmas holidays" and invited him to write the fourth in a series of books published by Girard "as a public service." He doesn't say, but the bank's publicity people do, that he was offered an undisclosed but substantial sum to write it. He wrote it over "the Christmas and New Year's holidays" and assumed when he did that he could properly and legally take the money because the work was done on his own time. After Buchanan delivered the manuscript to the bank, the propriety of his accepting the fee was questioned at the White House and the Justice Department. White House Counsel John Wesley Dean III, who has had such matters as the Watergate and related campaign scandals on his mind of late, and Justice Department lawyers ruled that Buchanan could properly and legally take the bank's money. When he was last heard from on the subject (he was at Harvard, addressing a seminar and out of reach by telephone when this report went to press), Buchanan was still trying to decide for himself whether to accept all or part of the fee.

Having absorbed and been chastened by Pat Buchanan's strictures against advocacy journalism, I wouldn't think of stating my opinion. According to the definition of advocacy journalism rendered on page 24 of *The New Majority,* if I did I would be acting "upon the belief that, given the facts, the American people are too ignorant to reach the proper conclusion and must be led there by the hand." This is what Buchanan says the majority of television network reporters and commentators do, and he is against them and it. He is also against journalists who write for print and commit the same sin, especially if their " 'biases and prejudices' are those of political 'liberalism.' " But it's the network reporters and commentators and their bosses who send Buchanan up the wall. His "Mr. Nixon and the Big Media" is the most interesting chapter in an interesting and lively book. It should remove any lingering doubt that the President and the Nixon officials concerned with media affairs believe that they have every right, constitutional and otherwise, to do everything in their power to whip and threaten and drive the offending media into line with the administration's notions of "comprehensiveness in coverage, objectivity in reporting, and balance in commentary."

Buchanan says, and his White House colleagues agree, that he wrote *The New Majority* on his own authority, without formal permission or clearance from the President or anybody else. He couldn't have been very apprehensive when he undertook to do it. He is the Nixon establishment's certified conservative philosopher, one of the last of the few genuine ideologues who entered the White House in 1969 with Mr. Nixon and the more characteristic and essentially uncommitted lawyers, advertising men, professional publicists and kindred pragmatists who dominate the place. Belief in Richard Nixon and whatever he professes to believe at any given moment is the White House norm. The atmosphere has never been really hospitable to true believers in something bigger than the man, whether they were Patrick Moynihan on the liberal left or Arthur Burns on the moderate right, and most of them are gone with Moynihan and Burns. Buchanan, a sometime newspaperman and staff speech writer, survives and thrives as a special consultant to the President and as an assistant without portfolio. He still works on occasional speeches. His principal chore, however, is just to be there, at the President's beck when he is wanted and in comforting touch with other conservatives who often feel, as Buchanan does, that Mr. Nixon harbors dangerously liberal tendencies that he must be cautioned and guarded against at all times. In *The New Majority,* for instance, there is a faint undertone of anxiety about the President's burgeoning accommodations with Soviet Russia and Communist China, a note of remindful doubt that they can be trusted to keep the disarmament and other agreements that Mr. Nixon has made with them and is trying to broaden. In the main, though, and certainly in his treatment of the media, Pat Buchanan bespeaks the true and controlling Nixon doctrine.

He correctly observes that many journalists acknowledge a predominantly "liberal" bias and counter such criticism as his by asking, "What else is new?" Buchanan answers: "What is new is not the existence of the liberal bias. What is new, in the last decade, is the wedding of that bias to unprecedented power. Men who are taking an increasingly adversary stance toward the social and political values, mores and traditions of the majority of Americans have also achieved monopoly control of the medium of communication upon which 60 percent of these Americans depend as the primary source of news and information about their government and society. And these men are using that monopoly position to persuade the nation to share their distrust of and hostility toward the elected government."

There is the sin in the Nixon-Buchanan view: "hostility toward the elected government." Pat Buchanan has a thing about elections and the elected. He attributes to "many network commentators and correspondents" a "claim to be the people's representatives in Washington" and derides it: "True 'representatives' of the people can be fired or rehired by the people at regular intervals—election time. To whom do the gentlemen of the networks answer, other than some nameless executive, whose principal concern is less the welfare of the nation, than the Nielsen ratings and profit margins?" In the hope that Pat will forgive a bit of advocacy here, I ask in return: to whom does he want them to answer—to incumbent and offended officialdom? He indicates that he doesn't, but my reading of him is that he does. I don't know how else to read the following passage: "Critics should not be distracted by cries of 'repression' and public tears over the 'death of the First Amendment.' Nothing in our Constitution, written or inherent, prevents individuals in government or private life from devising and proposing ways and means to crack this unprecedented concentration of political power, to open up the national airwaves, to guarantee that a broader range of information and opinion is brought before the American people." Buchanan doesn't repeat in explicit terms the suggestion that he once made in a television interview, to the effect that Congress or the executive branch might have to compel the networks by law or regulation to tailor reporting and commentary to the Nixon-Buchanan view of fairness and balance. He recommends, among other things, "a conscious search (by the networks) for newsmen and anchormen and commentators around the nation who feel and share the views and beliefs and the will to investigate and report and comment on the issues that most concern the American people—and not simply those of greatest interest to its Liberal Establishment." Pondering that dab of uncharacteristically muddy writing, one may doubt that Pat Buchanan has in mind vigorous investigation and reporting of such current issues as reviving inflation and the Republican campaign scandals.

Buchanan, who in person is a bright and sunny sort of man,

probably didn't mean to inject into his argument a note that is evident among some of his White House associates. It is a note of sheer envy and it emerges when Buchanan writes: "Not three men in the US Senate enjoy the celebrity status or wield the influence over American opinion of a Cronkite, a Sevareid, a Brinkley. Not even the elected President of the United States enjoys their nightly privilege of untrammeled access for their unchallenged views into twenty million American homes."

Remind me to notify Pat Buchanan when the networks refuse President Nixon access to those twenty million homes, in free prime time.

April 28, 1973

———

Buchanan neither accepted nor rejected the fee. The Girard Bank holds it in escrow, so to speak, until such time as Buchanan can accept it without embarrassment to him or Mr. Nixon.

XIII

A Touch of Pity

Pity for the President and for the Nixon men who are turning upon him and each other and in the process are destroying the White House establishment that I thought I had come to know pretty well in the past four years is not in fashion among my colleagues in the Nixon press corps. Nor among the few assistants who in late April were willing to talk with me about the rot of Watergate and what they think it is doing and is likely to do to the Nixon presidency. But it seems to me that a degree of compassion is in order. There is tragedy in the spectacle of a President demeaned, a presidency imperiled, and some awareness and recognition of it should be possible without condoning infamous conduct and without abetting the line of defense, now emerging at the White House, that any disclosure or comment that besmirches the President is a disservice to the country.

The attitudes discerned in the White House press room and in White House offices have more in common than one might expect. Among the reporters, the predominant note varies from subdued to ferocious satisfaction with the plight of a President whom most of us have always distrusted. The characteristic attitude toward White House staff and Cabinet types who in their time of ascendancy cloaked themselves in arrogant sanctimony and variously avoided, rebuffed, misled and abused the reporters who plagued them is typified by the journalist who remarked that he wouldn't be at all sorry to see some of these characters eating from metal trays in federal prisons. The essence of the staff attitudes toward the President and the senior assistants and advisers who are in trouble with him that I've encountered at middle and lower official levels is a somewhat more kindly but not altogether dissimilar mix of concern, disillusionment and anger.

Some recent Nixon history must be recalled in order to explain these attitudes. The erosion of the utter confidence in Mr. Nixon that once prevailed at the White House did not begin with Watergate and with the gradual disclosure of related thuggeries last summer and fall. It began with the President's treatment of his staff after his reelection last November. His cold demand for the immediate resignations of all of his assistants, at every level, and the even colder sorting out of those who could stay and those who had to leave were specifically expressed and implemented by the President's administrative chief, H. R. (Bob) Haldeman. But it was the President's doing; it was done at his command and in accordance with his declared wish to enter his second term with a reorganized and reinvigorated team. It was a brutal operation, but it was not the brutality in itself that had a permanent effect and left the surviving staff poorly prepared for the shock of the climactic Watergate and associated disclosures. The permanent and corrosive effect was from the demonstration that past loyalty to Richard Nixon did not ensure his loyalty in return. A doubt arose, a doubt that was sensed among the staff at the height of the reorganization last December and January but that I did not hear expressed in so many words in White House offices before mid-April. It was a doubt that Mr. Nixon really deserved the unswerving loyalty that in the first four years was the outstanding hallmark of his White House.

A quality worse than cruelty in its impact upon the staff was perceived in the way the reorganization was carried out. It was the quality of folly, a foolish and needless wasting of a priceless asset. Thus it was that the President's wisdom and judgment, in a sphere of intense and personal interest to his staff, were brought into question. It was noticed, too, that his closest and highest assistants, men such as Haldeman and John D. Ehrlichman, the assistant for domestic affairs, ordered and executed the reorganization with chilling enthusiasm and that in the course of it more power and status accrued to them. In all of this, quite apart from Watergate, there were the seeds of discontent and diminishing dedication to Richard Nixon.

One of the oddities of the President's Easter stay at his Florida home on Key Biscayne indicates his awareness not only of the current corrosion but of its roots in the events and reactions just described. Although Easter is not generally considered a season for the exchange of gladsome personal wishes, it was announced that on Easter morning the President telephoned several members of his staff in Washington "to wish them well." Among them were Haldeman, Ehrlichman and—of all people on the staff—White House Counsel John Wesley Dean III. Haldeman and Ehrlichman had deemed it necessary to hire a lawyer with whom, it was acknowledged in Florida after days of concealment, the President spent an hour in earnest and secret discussion at the White House on the previous Thursday. On that day, John Dean bypassed the White House press staff and issued from his own office a shattering statement to the effect that any White House associates who might hope or think that they could make him a Watergate scapegoat did not understand him and his implied readiness to tell all. The President himself, in a statement on the preceding Tuesday announcing his sudden discovery that Watergate was serious business and his readiness to suspend and dismiss any assistants who were indicted and convicted, indicated that Dean had been relieved of his responsibilities for investigating any possible White House involvement in the Watergate and concurrent scandals. In a mood of open contempt, Press Secretary Ronald Ziegler seemed to confirm the impression that Dean was tolerated but no longer usefully employed at the White House. The effect was to validate reported evidence that John Dean, the President's personal investigator, had been involved along with former Attorney General John Mitchell,

among others in Mr. Nixon's service and confidence, in the preliminaries to the Watergate burglary and bugging.

On the Tuesday after Easter, the President's notably uncommu-
nicative press staff confirmed a report that the President had telephoned Dean. The spokesman wouldn't confirm, but didn't have
the gall to deny, an accompanying report that Mr. Nixon had said
to John Dean, "You are still my counsel." The most the spokesman
would admit was that Dean was among the beleaguered assistants
to whom the President had conveyed his Easter regards. It was
the kind of reassurance of the President's affection and concern for
his staff that many on it, including the many who could have had
no part in or knowledge of the Watergate and kindred misdoings,
had been needing and wanting for quite a while. It came, unfor-
tunately for the effect that it might otherwise have had, from a
President who stood in sadly obvious need of all the loyalty and
protection he could command.

When Mr. Nixon flew back to Washington from Florida, he was
getting the opposite of that loyalty and protection. John Ehrlichman, who was more deeply involved in the 1972 campaign than
the press has generally discovered and since then has consistently
and publicly derided news reports of serious campaign misbehavior, said in an interview that he had argued last August for a
thorough investigation of the Committee for the Re-election of
the President. Clark MacGregor, who was then the committee
director, said this wasn't so. The man upon whom Ehrlichman
would have been duty bound to urge such an investigation was not
MacGregor but the President, and the inevitable effect of the spat
was to increase the spreading disbelief that Mr. Nixon could have
been as innocent of all that was going on around him and in his
behalf as he had said in August and continued to say he was.
Charles Colson, a former assistant who has resumed private law
practice in Washington with the President's fervent blessing, had
an associate put out the story that he, Colson, had warned Mr.
Nixon in January that some of his assistants were criminally involved and should be cleaned out of the White House. Colson
denied the story and the associate then explained the denial: good
old Chuck, as he used to be known at the White House, wouldn't
want it known that he had tried and failed in January to alert the

President to the "major developments" that the President is saying he wasn't aware of until or around March 21. It's an ugly business, it's going to be uglier, and I say again that I pity the President who suffers from it and, beyond denial or evasion now, is in part responsible for it. I also pity the country. After all, the Watergate mess could leave us with President Agnew.

May 5, 1973

———

It should be understood that the dates at the end of these pieces are the dates of *The New Republic* issues in which they appeared. The foregoing piece was written in the week preceding April 30.

XIV

From the Heart

President Nixon's darkest day yet, though predictably not the dark-est of his days to come, began with four resignations and two replacements and was supposed to end, but didn't, with a televised address in which he said he wanted to speak from his heart about "what has come to be known as the Watergate affair." When he concluded the address with "God bless America, and God bless every one of you," the television cameramen and technicians in his White House office thought they saw tears in his eyes. The Eco-nomic Stabilization Act was to expire at midnight and he signed a one-year extension of it. Alone and unannounced, he then walked from his office to the White House press room. There hadn't been time to turn on the lights over the podium. The President stood in the shadows and said to some 15 reporters and photographers: "Ladies and gentlemen of the press, we have had our differences in the past, and I hope you give me hell every time you think I'm wrong. I hope I'm worthy of your trust." Then he went to his quarters in the White House mansion and, it was said later, made and received several telephone calls. Whom he called and who called him was not announced. The inference was that his callers praised the speech and told the President that at long last he was atop the Watergate scandal and was going to come out of it clean and whole. If they told him that, they were wrong.

The resignations and replacements made this April 30 a day without precedent. Mr. Nixon listed them in a statement and again in the speech. Attorney General Richard G. Kleindienst, who had already withdrawn from the Watergate investigation because some of his friends and former associates were involved in it, had "asked to be relieved" and was resigning. Secretary of Defense Elliot L. Richardson, who had been at the Pentagon less than three months and had previously been secretary of Health, Education, and Welfare and undersecretary of State, would succeed Kleindienst and would immediately, before the Senate confirmed the new nomination, "assume full responsibility and authority for coordinating all federal agencies in uncovering the whole truth about this matter." The President said in the statement that "I have today accepted the resignations of two of my closest friends and most trusted assistants in the White House, H. R. Haldeman and John D. Ehrlichman," and in the speech he called them "two of the finest public servants it has been my privilege to know." He said in the statement, "I have today requested and accepted the resignation of John W. Dean III from his position on the White House staff as counsel." In the speech, without praise and without saying again that he had requested Dean's resignation, he simply and coldly said that Dean "has resigned." The final announcement was that his former law partner and since 1969 a special consultant on the White House staff, Leonard Garment, was succeeding Dean as White House counsel "until a permanent successor . . . is named" and would "represent the White House in all matters relating to the Watergate investigation."

Bob Haldeman was the chief of the White House staff, the guardian of the President's door and time and energies. John Ehrlichman, the assistant for domestic affairs, was the chief formulator and manager of domestic policy. Haldeman, a sometime advertising man, and Ehrlichman, a lawyer, entered the President's service in the 1950s and since 1969 had been at the controlling top and center of his White House establishment. Only Henry Kissinger for foreign affairs and, in a somewhat lesser degree, secretary of the Treasury George P. Shultz for economic policy and affairs, shared the confidence and affection of the President to the extent that Haldeman and Ehrlichman did. With their departure the Nixon White House that Washington and the country had known since 1969 would become a very different establishment and place. But not totally different, not as different as many supposed, and for a simple and obvious reason. The closed, secretive and often arrogant White House that they personified, and the way of conducting presidential business for which Haldeman and Ehrlichman were blamed and detested by many in Congress and elsewhere, were closed and secretive and arrogant because Richard Nixon wanted and required that kind of establishment and way. There's hope and talk around him now of opening up the White House processes and of his opening his door and himself to wider access than he permitted Bob Haldeman to permit. This predictably won't happen, not for long and not in any significant degree.

The reason it won't happen has to do with something more than Mr. Nixon's habits and nature. It has to do with a factor that was much in the public prints and mind during the President's first year or so in office and has faded from general awareness since then, thanks to Haldeman's stringent care of Mr. Nixon's time and energies. There is a limit to the President's energies and endurance, a point beyond which he loses adequate command of himself and his circumstances. He knows it. Haldeman knew it. The President's staff knew it and used to discuss it, in the course of praising and thanking Haldeman for the skill and effectiveness with which he took it into account and protected Mr. Nixon from excessive demands upon his time, patience and energies. The outward style and behavior of the Nixon White House may change with a new guardian at the door, new direction at the center just below the President. But the inner reality of the Nixon White House and the Nixon presidency is not likely to change, not so long as Richard Nixon is there to keep it as he wants and must have it.

The President said that in accepting the resignations of Haldeman and Ehrlichman he meant to leave "no implication whatever of personal wrongdoing on their part" and that Kleindienst has "no personal involvement whatever in this matter." He didn't say

anything like this about John Dean. He couldn't: it was too clear
from believable reports, some of them originating with Dean himself, that he was very much involved in the Watergate scandal and
in the effort over many months to conceal any White House involvement in it and related 1972 campaign espionage, sabotage
and misuse of huge sums of contributed cash. The concealment occurred and it could not have occurred without the knowledge and
collaboration of Haldeman and Ehrlichman. A fair question is
why Mr. Nixon—surely knowing as much now, however he may
insist that he knew nothing until late March—went to the lengths
he did to absolve Haldeman and Ehrlichman of any imputation of
involvement. Two reasons are evident. One is that they are certain
to be witnesses under oath in a Senate investigation and in the
courts and may be indicted defendants. Any statement by the
President that he knows them to be guilty of what they have been
and may be charged with would amount to conviction. Another
reason, not provably in the President's mind but certainly high in
the public mind, is that Bob Haldeman and John Ehrlichman are
among the appalling number of past and present subordinates and
associates of the President who soon will be required to say on
oath, in the courts and before Senator Sam Ervin's committee, that
Mr. Nixon did or didn't know what they knew and did or didn't
authorize or order them to do what they did and authorized.

Mr. Nixon said in his speech that he didn't know until March 21
and afterward "because I believed the reports I was getting" and
"because I had faith in the persons from whom I was getting them."
Two days after the resignations were accepted, *The New York
Times* reported in a convincingly circumstantial account that Haldeman, Ehrlichman, John Dean and former Attorney General John
Mitchell cooked up the reports that Mr. Nixon was getting, in a
preplanned and elaborate effort to cover up the truth and keep it
from the President. If they did keep the truth from him between
last June and March 21, as the President says somebody did, the
least and the best to be said of him is that they made a fool and
a dupe of him. Only a fool, a dupe, or a President who wanted the
proven truth to be kept from him could have, as he said, "dis-
counted the stories in the press that appeared to implicate members

of my administration or other officials of the campaign committee."
Discount, in any case, is not the truthful word. Mr. Nixon denounced the stories and the most persistent producer of them, *The
Washington Post,* privately and profanely in person and publicly
through his spokesman, Press Secretary Ronald Ziegler. On May 1,
in early evidence of superficial change at the White House, Ziegler
finally got around to apologizing for past denials and denunciations
to the *Post* and two of its reporters, Bob Woodward and Carl
Bernstein.

One must believe that Mr. Nixon spoke from the heart, as he
said he did, and bespoke his true self in his television address. He
said among other things: "We must maintain the integrity of the
White House. And that integrity must be real, not transparent.
There can be no whitewash at the White House." In a speech that
was of supreme importance to him, a speech that in its national
impact could go far toward determining whether he survives the
Watergate affair without resignation or impeachment, Mr. Nixon
did not maintain the integrity of the White House. He impaired it.
He evaded. He elided. He lied.

The President lied when he said: ". . . I decided as the 1972
campaign approached that the presidency should come first and
politics second. To the maximum extent possible, therefore, I
sought to delegate campaign operations, to remove the day-to-day
campaign decisions from the President's office and from the White
House." True enough, he said and pretended that he did this in
1972. It was a pretense then and it is a pretense now. During the
campaign and after he was reelected, working politicians on his
staff and at his Committee for the Re-election of the President told
me often, with pride and in detail, that he gradually moved from
a posture of some detachment in 1971 toward and finally, from
March of 1972 onward, into active direction of the campaign in
its major aspects. He publicly defended the interpretation of old
and new laws that permitted his agents to collect millions in un-
reported contributions. Through Charles Colson, a lawyer and
former assistant who is busily trying to qualify himself as a witness
rather than a defendant, the President directed and closely followed
the operations of the White House "attack group" that did much
to cut George McGovern down and keep him down. When the news

reports of Watergate and related scoundrelry seemed to threaten his reelection, Mr. Nixon directed and in effect dictated the most savage of the counterattacks. At the Republican convention in Miami Beach, Colson and John Ehrlichman ran the local Nixon show under daily, often hourly, orders from Bob Haldeman, who remained in Washington and at nearby Camp David with the President until the two of them flew to Florida and took personal charge.

"When I am the candidate, I run the campaign," Mr. Nixon said in January 1971. A good deal of his April 30 speech was devoted to maintaining that this wasn't true in 1972. It was true in 1972, his year of triumph and, it now appears, of potential ruin.

May 12, 1973

XV

Living with Henry

Henry Kissinger's return from his latest journey to Moscow was awaited by his staff with an interest that had nothing to do with the delay in arranging a firm date for Leonid Brezhnev's promised visit to Washington. The 132 people who comprise Kissinger's National Security Council establishment assumed that he would soon get around to telling them what some changes in the NSC staff structure that were announced last April 6 and decided upon well before then are going to mean to them and to their relationship with him and the President.

The patient acceptance of Kissinger's failure to tell even the senior members of his staff, including those who are directly affected, what he had in mind with the changes before or when they were announced, is a good indicator of how it is to work and live with Henry in the fifth year of that extraordinary experience. Sadly for reporters and commentators who in the past have made much of the horrors of working for Henry Kissinger, the horror stories are no longer told with horror. His secretive ways, his relentless demands for unattainable perfection, his occasional flashes of cutting anger have come to be taken for granted and dismissed with rather humorous pleas for understanding that it's Henry being Henry and doesn't really matter. Most of his 50 professional assistants are trained specialists with trained minds— career diplomats, economists, systems analysts, poltical scientists, a few lawyers and generalists. The plain fact, corny when baldly stated but nonetheless a fact, is that they perceive in Kissinger the possessor of a superlative mind who stretches their minds and capabilities to the utmost and, along with the pains and passing resentments, gives them a profound sense of satisfaction and reward when he does it.

The changes in staff structure reflect Kissinger's evolution in the job since he became Mr. Nixon's assistant for national security affairs in 1969. It took him 18 months to come around to acceptance of one subordinate with the title and status of deputy assistant to the President. Now he is to have four subordinates with that title and a fifth with the status but not the title. Kissinger's mix of reasons for such a generous expansion of a rank that confers upon the holders, in theory though not necessarily in fact, the prestige of responsibility to the President rather than to him provides an interesting insight into his evolving view of his job and of the NSC function.

The reason of greatest general interest, though not the most immediate and important reason to be stated in forthcoming explanations to the staff, is that Kissinger is preparing the NSC structure for his departure. He is aware that his associates are basing their own plans on the assumption that he will be around for two years and probably no more than two years of the second Nixon term. He neither questions nor discourages the assumption. But his present intention could change for one or more of several reasons. The President could lose confidence in him; he could lose confidence in the President; or an impossible situation for him could be created by the replacement of the docile and cooperative William P. Rogers with a secretary of State, John Connally for instance, who would not tolerate Kissinger's ascendancy in the formulation and execution of foreign policy. One thing that certainly will not happen, I am assured and believe, is Kissinger's departure because of the Watergate scandal and the imputations of involvement that now crowd upon the President. The consensus around Kissinger is that, all other considerations apart, he will not desert the President at a time when his departure would be interpreted as a show of distrust. If it ever comes to a matter of nonconfidence on either man's part, it will be over issues of policy principle and that is extremely improbable. Eventual departure is a factor in the structural changes only in the sense that Kissinger wants to leave behind him, when and if he goes, an NSC system and NSC procedures that are not as dependent upon him as they have been and that a successor can operate with until he rearranges the setup to suit himself.

Kissinger's principal purpose, as it will be explained to the staff, is to make it easier to work with him and for him to work with his assistants. As I get the story, he realized many months ago that he had become a bottleneck in the system and that the single deputy assistant, originally General Alexander M. Haig, Jr., and now Brigadier General Brent Scowcroft, had become another bottleneck. In the intensely personalized procedure that Kissinger started with in 1969 and has dominated since then, policy business that he didn't have the time to handle was supposed to be handled by the deputy and neither of them had enough time to do it. This became acutely obvious at the height of the negotiations for an Indochina and Vietnam settlement last year, when both Kissinger and General Haig were frequently abroad, and Kissinger finally brought himself to do something about it with the designation of a "deputy for operations." His choice for the job is Lawrence S. Eagleburger, aged 43, a career foreign service officer who worked himself into physical breakdown as a personal assistant to Kissinger in 1969 and lately has been acting assistant secretary of Defense for international security affairs. Kissinger's theory is that a few hours a week with Eagleburger, imparting to him Kissinger's and the President's views and wishes, will qualify the new deputy to act for Kissinger on marginal matters and serve as a buffer between him and senior members of the staff. The hope is that this will allow Kissinger ample time, more time than he has had in the past, for personal discussion with his senior associates and their juniors on critical matters. Such is the theory. One of Kis-

singer's oldest and most loyal associates advised me to assume that the theory won't work out. Henry's insistence upon personal and minute supervision of everything that concerns him and the President will never change, this fellow said, adding that the demands of the staff for personal contact with Henry will never change, either.

The two other new deputies (for "planning" and for international economic affairs) are to be Colonel Richard T. Kennedy, a retired army officer who since 1969 has been the staff planning director, and Charles A. Cooper, a former Rand Corporation economist who since 1970 has been the chief economics officer at the US Embassy in Saigon. The "planning" in Colonel Kennedy's old and new titles is something of a euphemism. A quiet man with a passion for orderly labor, he keeps the otherwise frantic NSC pace and procedure in a condition bearably short of chaos and, in simple justice, had to be accorded the higher title and status if anybody was. Charles Cooper, an eminent economist in his own right, gets the rank because he probably couldn't have been recruited without it. His advent signals Kissinger's determination to have the NSC staff play a larger and more effective role in international economic policy than it previously has. Philip Odeen, the NSC staff's chief systems analyst, gets the status without the title for one of those curious reasons that often operate in officialdom. His opposite number at the Department of Defense was recently downgraded, and Kissinger figured that he couldn't formally upgrade Odeen without offending the powers at DOD.

A victim and beneficiary of the same sort of official quirkery is Helmut Sonnenfeldt, who since 1969 has been Kissinger's senior specialist on Soviet and East European affairs. Sonnenfeldt, a foreign service officer, is credited with immense contributions to the President's Moscow summit, strategic arms negotiations, the whole range of widening accommodation with the Soviet Union. By acknowledged right, he should have been designated Kissinger's senior deputy. But—and here I repeat what I'm told—many of Hal Sonnenfeldt's associates find him impossibly difficult to work for. Kissinger concluded that he would have a staff revolt and unmanageable chaos on his hands if he gave Sonnenfeldt the promotion he had earned. The department of State didn't want him back. Elliot Richardson, who thought he was staying at the Defense Department and instead has been named attorney general in the forlorn hope that he can clear up and sanitize the Watergate scandal, rejected Kissinger's urgent recommendation that Sonnenfeldt be appointed assistant secretary for international security affairs. Ostensibly Richardson refused on the mentioned personality grounds. Actually, as Richardson saw it, the issue was whether the White House should or shouldn't dictate DOD appointments. So Kissinger worked the problem out with Treasury Secretary George Shultz and Hal Sonnenfeldt is to be an undersecretary of the Treasury, specializing in international economic affairs. He's happy and Kissinger is happy.

This is one of the few occasions for happiness at the beleaguered White House. Another one, in NSC quarters, is the fact that General Haig has temporarily replaced H. R. Haldeman as Mr. Nixon's chief of staff. Haldeman detested Kissinger and Kissinger detested Haldeman. Grave and growing concern that Watergate is eroding the President's authority abroad as well as at home outweighs all other considerations in Henry Kissinger's vicinity. But one hears it said in that vicinity, though not by Kissinger, that if any good could come of Watergate it was the removal of Bob Haldeman and his California crowd from power at the White House.

May 19, 1973

———

I should have but didn't realize when the preceding piece was written that Kissinger already had cause to hope and expect that he could become secretary of State without giving up his White House position. I was sap enough to fall for his plaintive protestations, then and later, that only a fool would want to be secretary of State. Hal Sonnenfeldt was outraged by my account of how he came to be shunted to the Treasury. Because of outrageous rightist objections to his confirmation as Treasury undersecretary, he joined Kissinger at the State Department in early 1974.

A Searing Wound

One of the few White House assistants who has seen enough of the President in recent weeks to have a worthwhile impression of his mood and manner in private said the other day that Mr. Nixon reminds him of a man who has suffered "a searing wound" —here the assistant swept his right hand across his belly—and is trying to live with and forget the unforgettable pain. Another assistant who has spent a good deal of time with the President said that Mr. Nixon appeared to him to be going through one trauma after another, "peeling off layer after layer and finally getting down to the bitter core of truth."

They were talking, of course, about the pain and the truth of Watergate. It will be observed that such accounts (any accounts at all of Mr. Nixon's private and actual attitude in this time of crisis and dissolution are hard to come by) serve a central White House purpose. The purpose is to support and further the story that the President knew nothing about the evils that "Watergate" has come to encompass until, as he has said, the truth about them began to crash in upon him last March 21. My own belief is that it was not knowledge of the wrongs done by men around him and in his behalf that began to crash in upon him then. It was, the mounting evidence indicates to me, recognition that the involvement of men whose whole aim in life and office was to serve him and do his bidding could not be hidden much longer. Proof that this is so is yet to appear and may never appear. But accounts of the kind to be summarized in this report must be rendered and read, it seems to me, with the assumption that the overwhelming necessity recognized by Mr. Nixon in late March and now driving him and his shaken White House establishment is to save his presidency. Not *the* presidency, let it be noted, but *this* presidency. The institution is safe. This President is not.

A part of the bitter truth acknowledged and acted upon April 30 by the President was that two of his three closest assistants, H. R. Haldeman and John D. Ehrlichman, had to be let go. Much of the available story of how Mr. Nixon has dealt with his situation and reacted to it has to do with his and their behavior in the time just before and just after he accepted and announced their resignations. The news reports that Haldeman and Ehrlichman spent their last days in favor and power fighting for their jobs appear in the aftermath to have been only a portion of the larger and more interesting truth that Mr. Nixon spent the same days fighting to keep them in their jobs. Their functional importance to him and to the Nixon presidency, Haldeman as chief and monitor of the entire White House staff and Ehrlichman as the principal domestic adviser, was sufficient reason but by no means the whole reason for him to cling to them. Richard Nixon trusts very few people and he trusted them. They were his friends, and his true and accepted friends are few. It appears now that much of his and their time in happier days was passed in easy talk, hours of it in the intimacy that this most secluded and private of Presidents requires and cannot readily attain. He and they realized, too, that their resignations, however cushioned they might be in the terms of the announcement, would be interpreted as implied admissions of grave wrong and guilt, certainly theirs and possibly his.

Men still in Mr. Nixon's service and others who have served other Presidents say it is inconceivable to them that Haldeman and Ehrlichman should not have said to the President, at some point between late March and the final weekend of decision, that they were prepared to go if he concluded that it was in his interest for them to go. If they did, the fact is unknown to anyone except him and them or, if known to anyone else, has not been divulged. By April 20, when Mr. Nixon repaired from Washington to his Florida home, he had all but concluded that he would have to reject their pleas that they should remain in his service for his and their good. It seemed apparent to him that his statement of April 17 that any White House assistant or any other official in his administration who was proven to have been involved in the Watergate and related scandals would be dismissed and punished in the courts, without hindrance from him, was not enough to quiet suspicion and still the clamor. The few assistants who had some guide to his thinking expected him to announce the resignations when he returned to Washington on April 24. Instead he let Haldeman and Ehrlichman renew their pleas and considered once again an alternative to resignation that he was thought to have discarded. This was that he grant them leaves of absence, without prejudice to them, in hope that they could survive the coming storms and return to the White House; or, if that proved to be impossible, at least defer the onus upon them and him of outright and immediate resignation. Mr. Nixon was still pondering that choice and seeking justifications for it when he took Haldeman and Ehrlichman with him on a brief ceremonial trip to Mississippi. It was only when he returned and retired for the weekend to his mountain retreat at Camp David that he let himself be persuaded again that anything short of immediate resignations would merely prolong the agony and compound the suspicion that he was protecting Haldeman and Ehrlichman in order to protect himself. It is said at the White House that they were still pleading for mercy and time when the President summoned them to Camp David and told them that he was announcing their resignations in a statement the next morning and in a speech that night.

The night of April 30 and the following day, May 1, are remembered at the White House as the absolute low points of the Nixon presidency to date. Mr. Nixon appeared to be shattered, uncertain, confused. A Cabinet meeting the afternoon of May 1 was a depressing affair for all who were there. "He was not at his best" is the most charitable summation of it that I've heard. His reminder that "we have had our Cambodia" and survived it conveyed a sense of more pathos than confidence. He told his Cabinet that Kenneth Cole, who had replaced John Ehrlichman as executive director of the Domestic Council in December, would hereafter be expected to manage and coordinate communication between the President and department heads. Beyond that, he seemed to be groping for ways to fill the huge administrative gap left by the resignations of Haldeman and Ehrlichman. Afterward, he spent a rare hour with Vice President Agnew and had it announced that he expected the Vice President to play a larger and more aggressive part in the business of the Domestic Council and in the shaping of domestic policy than he had previously been encouraged or allowed to play. Agnew at this writing is still awaiting solid evidence that anything much will come of the mandate. Kenneth Cole has conferred with him a few times. There have been some token gestures toward consultation with him on domestic programs and legislation. A Nixon spokesman indicated that Agnew as vice chairman of the Domestic Council would be an active and important figure around the White House from then on. The Domestic Council last met on December 6, 1971. Its work is done in small committees and by staff groups, and there is a detectable lack of enthusiasm for bringing the Vice President and his recently reduced staff into this activity in any regularized and effective way.

The first evidence that the President was snapping back from his depression was the reappearance at the White House of General Alexander M. Haig, Jr., who had been Henry Kissinger's deputy on the NSC staff and in January had become the army's vice chief of staff. Mr. Nixon brought him back to replace Bob Haldeman for a while, pull the battered White House staff together and study ways in which it might be reorganized. The President then flew off to Florida again, and the testimony of his assistants is that the stay did wonders for him. What probably did the most for him was a visit with John B. Connally, the Nixocrat who had just turned Republican and celebrated the event with a trip to Key Biscayne. Connally agreed to join the White House staff as a part-time, unpaid "special adviser." He stuck to the agreement after a barrage of press inquiries about the manifest conflict between his interests as a Texas lawyer for oil and other businesses and his policy role at the White House forced him to withdraw from his law firm and from sundry corporate boards. It's assumed at the White House that Connally will have a major role both in policy formulation and in reorganizing the place. No doubt he will, but my guess is that Mr. Nixon wanted and invited him back because he's somebody the President can talk to with confidence and in intimacy, thus filling that part of the need once met by Haldeman and Ehrlichman. If the Nixon-Connally partnership also promotes John Connally's hopes of being the next President, so much the better and so much the worse (Mr. Nixon must reflect) for Vice President Agnew.

The same sort of press-room carping that dogged Connally out of his law firm and directorships hastened the final departure of Bob Haldeman and John Ehrlichman. They continued to turn up, between appearances before a grand jury and sessions with the staff of Senator Ervin's Watergate investigating committee. They stayed on the payroll. They used White House cars. Ehrlichman still had the use of his West Wing office (General Haig had moved into Haldeman's office, and Haldeman was said to have temporary quarters in the Executive Office Building next door). What they did at the White House, before the daily questions raised about them in the press room led to the announcement that they went off the payroll on May 18, was something of a mystery. The little learned about it makes a sad story. FBI and Secret Service agents guarded their files. Bob Haldeman, lately second only to the President in prestige and power, had to submit to searches before he left his temporary office. When he wanted to dictate some memorandum notes for one of his grand jury appearances, he was required to let a Secret Service agent listen. It was said that Haldeman was visibly hurt but took it well. John Ehrlichman spent some of his last days and hours at the White House in conference with Kenneth Cole, advising him on how to handle his expanded functions as a coordinator of domestic affairs and as a communicator between the President and the heads of domestic departments and agencies. Mr. Nixon let it be known that he expects hereafter to deal directly with his Cabinet secretaries in a way he never has.

But it is well understood at the White House that Cole and the five assistant directors of the Domestic Council are to handle most of the President's business with the concerned departments and agencies. Mr. Nixon expects future demands upon his limited time and patience to be held pretty much to the prudent minimum that they have been held to in the past.

Watergate and its associated troubles didn't go away, of course. Henry Kissinger, hitherto immune, was discovered to have tolerated and used, if he didn't request, FBI taps on the telephones of some of his NSC assistants. This was neither as scandalous nor as extraordinary as news accounts made it appear and it caused very little surprise and discomfiture within the NSC staff. But the disclosure disturbed Kissinger and contributed its bit to the dominant note at the Nixon White House in mid-May. It was a note of apprehension, of deepening awareness that the worst of Watergate is yet to come and that Richard Nixon cannot be as certain as he wants to appear to be that he and his presidency can survive it.

May 26, 1973

XVII

A Limited Confession

At the end of the sadly incomplete confession and plea for belief and understanding that Mr. Nixon issued on May 22, in his third attempt within five weeks to save himself and his presidency from the ruin that the Watergate scandals threaten, he gave an indication of the dilemma in which he is trapped and of the atmosphere of doubt and distrust in which he is fighting for survival. He did this when, after saying that the longer of two statements issued in his name was limited to his recollections of what he had said and done, he added: "I have specifically avoided any attempt to explain what other parties may have said and done. My own information on these matters is fragmentary, and to some extent contradictory. Additional information may be forthcoming of which I am unaware."

Mr. Nixon must be assumed to know a great deal about Watergate that he said he didn't know. One thing he knew was that he dared not make and defend his statements in person at a press conference and expose himself to the many questions that they raised. His press secretary said that he intends to have a news conference "in the very near future." But he chose on the 22nd, after much thought and private debate among the few assistants to whom he entrusted the preparation of the statements, to remain in seclusion when they were produced in the White House press room and to have two White House lawyers, Leonard Garment and J. Fred Buzhardt (pronounced buzzert), justify and explain the President's account for him as best they could. It was a poor best. The main reason it was had very little to do with the care for "national security" and for the rights of jeopardized individuals that the President asserted and that his lawyers adduced in a clamorous bout with reporters. To state the reason is to define the essence of Mr. Nixon's dilemma. It is that he and his lawyers are not sure that they know what some of the "other parties" to whom he referred are prepared and going to say under oath, in peril of perjury, when they testify in the courts and before Senator Ervin's investigating committee.

The fact that the President and his lawyers are not sure about this is a testament to the truly horrible atmosphere that prevailed behind the scenes at the Nixon White House in late May. The "other parties" in question include former Attorney General John N. Mitchell, former Commerce Secretary Maurice Stans, and former White House assistants H. R. Haldeman, John D. Ehrlichman, Charles Colson. One would suppose that such friends and devotees of the President would long since have come clean with him and with the several lawyers who are helping him prepare his own case and his own defense before the bar of public opinion and, conceivably though as yet improbably, before the Senate in impeachment proceedings. One would suppose that the President by May 22 surely knew the worst that awaits him in the testimony of the five men just named and of the several others who once served him and will be saying that he has or hasn't told the truth. Haldeman and Ehrlichman continued to occupy White House offices and were at his call through the weekend preceding the statements. Charles Colson has been in and out of the Executive Office Building next door to the White House. Maurice Stans was seen

in an EOB corridor on the afternoon of May 21, hours after he
had been arraigned for trial in New York, drawn and tense and
visibly suffering, walking toward the EOB office frequently used
by Mr. Nixon. Garment, Buzhardt, other staff lawyers and the
President himself have questioned all of those who may imperil
the President and who have been willing to talk. Some of them
have not been willing or, if willing, have left an impression that
they were less than frank. For whatever reason, I am believably
told that despite these intense inquiries since late March the President is not certain and feels that he cannot be certain that he knows
the worst. He and the assistants who have been exploring the
Watergate ramifications with and for him do know that the full
extent of the felonies, political espionage, illegal collection and
misuse of campaign funds, and other abuses perpetrated in his behalf by people who thought they were doing what he wanted done
is yet to be revealed. The May 22 statements were framed to allow
for the anticipated worst in the way of behavior that is yet to be
and is expected to be disclosed. But, excepting the kind of precau-
tionary and qualifying language quoted at the start of this report,
the statements could not be framed to allow for possible testimony
that, for all the President knows, may make him appear to be a
multiple liar.

A measure of Mr. Nixon's desperation is the fact that he deliberately took this risk in both of the May 22 statements. In a brief
summary statement, pointing up his longer and more detailed account of what he called "my own recollections of what I said and
did," he denied that he did or condoned seven specific things.
Each of these denials is subject to dispute and, with each of them,
the President took the chance that no credible witness will dispute
them and so open him to the charge and, inevitably in the minds
of many, the belief that he lied in the course of pleading for belief.
Omitting the numbers that he attached to each of the seven denials,
they follow as he stated them: "I had no prior knowledge of the
Watergate operation. I took no part in, nor was I aware of, any
subsequent efforts that may have been made to cover up Watergate. At no time did I authorize any offer of executive clemency
for the Watergate defendants, nor did I know of any such offer. I
did not know, until the time of my own investigation, of any effort

to provide the Watergate defendants with funds. At no time did I attempt, or did I authorize others to attempt, to implicate the CIA in the Watergate matter. It was not until the time of my own investigation that I learned of the break-in at the office of Mr. [Daniel] Ellsberg's psychiatrist, and I specifically authorized the furnishing of this information to Judge Byrne. I neither authorized nor encouraged subordinates to engage in illegal or improper campaign tactics." It is upon the validity of these denials, and upon the credibility of testimony likely to bring some if not all of them into question, that Mr. Nixon must stand or fall.

Mr. Nixon confessed to several things that he has previously denied or, stating the point in the gentlest possible way, previously concealed. He confessed that he instituted in 1969 a series of domestic surveillance procedures, varying from wiretapping to felonious physical intrusion upon property and privacy, that were put to illegal and improper political uses before and during his 1972 campaign for relection. He confessed that he ordered senior White House assistants, his attorney general and the directors of various intelligence services to restrict investigation of the Watergate bugging and burglary that set off the sequence of disastrous disclosures last June. His excuse—the central point of his defense—is that he demanded restriction but not a cover-up in order to protect intelligence procedures that he considers vital to national security. Whatever wrong was done in this cause, including the illegal dragging of the Central Intelligence Agency into domestic surveillance, he attributed to zealous officials who variously misunderstood him and his orders, concealed much of what they were doing from him, and continually reassured him that nobody in his White House establishment was doing or had done anything wrong. He got closest to genuine confession in the ordinary meaning of the word when he said: "With hindsight, it is apparent that I should have given more heed to the warning signals I received along the way about a Watergate cover-up and less to the reassurances." The weakness of his account leaped from a betraying phrase in a reference to his 1972 campaign. "It is clear," he said, "that unethical as well as illegal activities took place in the course of that campaign. None of these took place with my specific knowledge or approval." A President who was as innocent of knowledge and involvement as Mr. Nixon claimed to be would not have had to have his lawyers and drafters write that none of it took place with his *specific* knowledge and approval.

June 21, 1973

XVIII

Kissinger & Haig

This piece is about two men in the President's service, Henry Kissinger and General Alexander M. Haig, Jr., whom I have admired in the past without serious reservation. In my opinion, they continue to serve Mr. Nixon and through him the country in necessary and useful ways at a time when he and the country need all the help that's available. At the moment and specifically, they are doing what they appear to believe they honorably can do to help the President survive the Watergate scandals and, while doing this, diminish the stain from those scandals that inevitably touches them. The fact that it touches them is in itself evidence and a part of the encompassing Watergate tragedy. What follows is an effort to place their roles in a perspective that does them justice without minimizing the enormous offense against the public good and against decency in the public service that Watergate in its totality constitutes.

It must be said that the offense is compounded by everyone, beginning with the President and including Kissinger and Haig among others at the White House, who in whatever ways and for whatever reasons tries to obscure and narrow adequate understanding of what the varied evils now labeled "Watergate" involve and signify. That is precisely what the President, Kissinger, Haig and the few other assistants who are trusted and relied upon at the seat of the endangered Nixon presidency are trying to do. No absolution for that effort and the distortions of fact and understanding that result from it is offered here. The sole points to be made in behalf of the immediate subjects, Kissinger and Haig, in their current roles as the President's defenders are that they and others in more or less equivalent positions at the White House must do what they are doing so long as they choose to serve a President who clings to his office as Mr. Nixon is clinging to his; and that, on the basis of the facts known at this writing, they do not deserve the worst of the hard time they are getting in much of the Watergate reporting and comment.

Because General Haig is the lesser known of the two, we begin with him. He is a professional soldier and he was an army colonel when, at age 44, he joined Kissinger's National Security Council staff in 1969 after tours at the Defense Department and at West Point. In four years the President promoted him to brigadier and major general and, last January, jumped him past the three-star grade of lieutenant general to four-star rank and made him the army's vice chief of staff. During the four years of Haig's NSC duty, the last 30 months of it as Kissinger's only deputy assistant for national security affairs, I never heard anything but good about Haig from the harried assistants, nearly all of them civilians, who labored under the Kissinger lash and found in Colonel and General Haig a capacity for calm and orderly performance under pressure that Kissinger notoriously lacks. Mr. Nixon evidently found a good deal more in Haig: he alone among Kissinger's associates came to share the President's confidence and to be consulted by him in matters of high policy in anything like the degree that Henry Kissinger shared it and was consulted.

In retrospect, however, one perceives qualities in Haig that a former cadet who had some dealings with him at West Point, where Haig was a regimental commander and deputy commandant, describes in admittedly hostile fashion in a recent issue of the *Village Voice*. The sometime cadet is Lucian K. Truscott IV, grandson of a famous World War II general and son of a career army officer. Beneath Haig's "charisma and leadership ability," Cadet Truscott detected "a compulsive desire to keep everything within the regiment," including rampant marijuana smoking and honor code violations, and an absolute regard for vested authority and sanctity of orders. Soon after Haig was recalled from the Pentagon to replace discarded H. R. Haldeman as the President's administrative chief of staff at the White House, I heard stories about him in his earlier NSC role that seem to reflect some of the qualities noted by Truscott. At the time of the Cambodia invasion in 1970, when several of Kissinger's assistants quit, Haig in his rage and disgust showed a dismaying inability to grasp or acknowledge the possibility that good men might put principle above orders and higher authority. The NSC resignations occurred for a variety of reasons, objection to the Cambodia operation among them but not in most instances the primary cause. Even so, they didn't justify the harsh and critical reaction from Haig that some of the victims now recount. Truscott concludes in his savage memoir that Haig as the President's White House administrator is ideally suited to the obfuscation and concealment of past wrongs that the job requires and may be better at it than Bob Haldeman was. To me, the chief significance of Haig's return to the White House is its evidence of the President's pathetic shortage of people whom he trusts and to whom he can turn in a time of extreme need. Something is said about the President's plight when he has to deprive the army of its vice chief of staff and install a four-star general in a job that a military man simply shouldn't be doing. Still more is said when Mr. Nixon has to look for excuses to keep General Haig in an essentially political and civilian function for at least a year because nobody else with his recognized skills and reputation for integrity is known and available to the President.

One of General Haig's recent duties has been to urge upon certain reporters and commentators the view that the domestic surveillance, wiretapping and related measures that the President has confessed to instituting in 1969 really have nothing to do with the overall Watergate scandals in which these activities have become enmeshed and should not only be distinguished from the Watergate evil but justified on the ground that they were as necessary for "national security" as Mr. Nixon said they were on May 22. Columnist Joseph Kraft's assertion the other day that Haig in the process "has been blackening reputations and disclosing the contents of wiretaps—itself a violation of the law" was excessive and may have been based upon misinformation. But General Haig's White House assignment opens him to the charge and, at the least, makes him by definition a participant in and abettor of the President's transparent effort to cloak himself and his stingily acknowledged responsibility for the Watergate climate in the camouflage of national security.

Now for Henry Kissinger and his part in the same endeavor. My sympathies are with Kissinger and not with the whining complaint that the NSC assistants whose home telephones were tapped in the course of the aforementioned surveillance operations were outrageously imposed upon in violation of their civil and personal rights. People who hold NSC and similar staff jobs at the core of national security policy formulation—and there are compelling considerations of national security, despite the President's protective abuse of them—waive normal rights to personal privacy. Competent professionals in such jobs understand this and accept the occasional consequences. The acknowledged tapping of four journalists' phones that also occurred between 1969 and early 1971 is a different affair, but there could be and perhaps were justifying reasons for that as well. All of which is prelude to my view that Henry Kissinger mishandled but did not disqualify himself when the issue was raised by disclosure of the taps on some of his assistants. He dissimulated, he equivocated, he came mighty close to lying as Joe Kraft asserted he did, before he finally got around to saying publicly on May 28 that "my office supplied [to the FBI] the names of some of the individuals who had access to the information that was being investigated" and adding: "I am responsible for what happens in my office and I won't give the names of the people who did it." The man who did it for Kissinger was Haig. Both of them were acting on the President's authority and both of them, in the sense already indicated, must share with him some of the responsibility for the White House climate that produced Watergate.

June 9, 1973

———

This piece pained Kissinger, enraged Haig, and inspired Anthony
Lewis, a *New York Times* columnist, to denounce in *The New
Republic* my toleration of NSC taps.

XIX

Toughing It Out

On Sunday evening, June 10, at Homestead Air Force Base near Miami, Mr. Nixon was seen to do something that I hadn't seen him do in five years of watching him get on and off airplanes. He usually trots up the steep ramps, without pause. This time he put his left hand on the rail of the ramp leading from the tarmac to the door of Air Force One and pulled himself up, pausing for a split second after every two or three steps. Mrs. Nixon walked beside him, pacing her climb with his. At the top of the ramp, the President turned and waved with his customary show of vigor. Then he and his wife vanished and their plane took off for Washington, routinely ending another of the President's frequent weekends of mingled rest and work at his home on Key Biscayne.

On the way from Washington to Key Biscayne, on the preceding Friday, the President made a speech. It was his first appearance at a fully open and public gathering since he was reelected last November. His evident purpose was to demonstrate that the Watergate scandals and repercussions didn't scare him and that he'd meant it when he said on May 22: "I will not abandon my re-

sponsibilities. I will continue to do the job I was elected to do."
His audience of graduates, students, parents and miscellaneous
citizens on the campus of Florida Technological University, a
regional institution that opened in 1968 and was having its fourth
commencement ceremony, expected Mr. Nixon to talk about Watergate. Florida Tech is a conservative school in a conservative area.
Reporters in the President's press party were told that he'd have
got a thunderous ovation if he'd chosen to say that he'd done no
wrong and to hell with anybody who said he had. He chose instead
to dump a bag of Nixon clichés dating back to and before his
1968 campaign, along with references to peaceful accommodation
with Communist China and the Soviet Union and a strong suggestion that people bring inflation on themselves by "living better" and
increasing their demands for meat, grain, coal, gasoline, fuel oil,
electricity and air conditioners. He was applauded 14 times in 28
minutes, with audibly diminishing enthusiasm. His single and
oblique reference to Watergate, with never a mention of the word,
occurred in a passage that is quoted at length because it's vintage
Nixon syntax and all, and because it's manifestly what the President thought it useful and appropriate to say at this time on this
occasion. After remarking that commencement speakers usually go
to extremes of pessimism or optimism, Mr. Nixon said:

"I am going to try to avoid both extremes and be quite candid
with you today about your opportunities and also the problems.
But in view of the fact that there is somewhat of a tendency to
have our television sets inundated with what is wrong with America, which, of course, is their responsibility where they feel that,
I think perhaps it would be well to start with this proposition:
about what is perhaps right about this country, and I would say
we have grave problems at home and abroad, and we are capable
of solving them. But I want you to know that I have visited most
of the countries of the world. I have seen most of the systems of
government of the world, and I have lived through four wars that
America has been engaged in in this century. I can say very hon-
estly to every member of this graduating class: If I were to pick
a time in the whole history of the world in which to live, if I were
to pick a country in which I would like to live in all this world,
there is no country I would rather live in and there is no time I

would rather be graduating from college than 1973, the United States of America."

After repeating at the end that "in the whole history of the world, in all the nations of the world, there has never been a time when I would rather be a graduate than in the year 1973 in the United States of America," the President walked from the platform to the area below it where the graduates were seated. Reporters who trailed him noticed an odd reaction when some of the graduates shouted "we believe in you" and "we're behind you." These and similar cries of encouragement could be interpreted only as reminders of Watergate and they seemed to bother and irritate Mr. Nixon. Although he muttered "thank you" once or twice, he looked as if he were anything but grateful and wanted to get away from the people whom he had sought out. At the air force base where his plane awaited him, he approached a small crowd of onlookers and shook a few hands and said "thank you" when somebody shouted, "You're still on top." He had that same look of distaste and irritation when he told the crowd, "I've got to catch the helicopter" and strode toward Air Force One, which is not a helicopter.

Mr. Nixon returned from Florida to a White House establishment that he is changing in many respects but can't change in one important respect so long as he "toughs it out" (as Senator John Stennis of Mississippi correctly predicted he would do not long ago). He's the same President now that he was between January 20, 1969, and April 30, 1973, when he sadly announced the resignations of H. R. Haldeman, his administrative staff chief, and John D. Ehrlichman, his assistant for domestic affairs, because of their deep entanglements in the multiple Watergate rascalities. The tight, secretive and centralized system of White House command that they created for him and, at his behest, brought to a peak of perverted perfection in the months between his reelection and the bursting of the Watergate bomb in late March was the sort of system that suited him, that he wanted, and that he conceived and developed through them. Whatever changes he is compelled to make, and however extensive their outward effect may be, it should never be forgotten that the system he is professing to discard was the kind that he thought he needed if he was to conduct his presidency in his chosen way. The changes in staff personnel and organization that he is making, in the hope that they will help him escape resignation or impeachment, can be really effective only if Mr. Nixon changes, and that seems to me to be extremely doubtful.

The reporters and cameramen who witnessed the first display of the staff changes on June 6 will never forget it. One of the reporters who tried to convey the weird effect in words gave up and said afterward, "You can't describe it; you have to have been there and seen it." Here, in little hope that the effect of seeing it will be conveyed, is what happened. Mr. Nixon appeared on the West Wing porch outside his Oval Office with former Congressman and Defense Secretary Melvin Laird and General Alexander M. Haig, Jr., at his right and left. They paused for pictures on the steps that lead down into the Rose Garden, then walked the grassy length of the garden and wheeled to face the cameras again. They murmured to each other, smiled at each other, and walked back through the garden to the porch and into the Oval Office. On the porch steps, Mr. Nixon reached up and patted General Haig's right shoulder. It was done in total silence. Something about the scene, perhaps nothing more than its staged artificiality, made the watching reporters nervous. One of them said in a shaken tone, "I guess it's to show that Nixon is up and taking nourishment." Another said, "I don't believe it. It didn't happen." Why we felt that way, I don't know and probably never will.

A written announcement awaited us in the press room. It said that General Haig, who had been Henry Kissinger's deputy and had been appointed army vice chief of staff in January, "will retire from active duty in the Army effective August 1." A great fuss had been raised about a career soldier replacing Haldeman in a basically civilian job, handling (as the announcement put it) "coordination and supervision of the day-to-day operations and responsibilities of the White House staff." Melvin Laird, who had resigned as Defense secretary in January and within the past two weeks had sworn to reporters that he wouldn't return to government, was appointed "Counsellor to the President for Domestic Affairs . . . responsible for overall formulation and coordination of domestic policy." He would have Cabinet rank, which John Ehrlichman hadn't enjoyed, and he would "also sit on the National Security

Council," as Ehrlichman never had. Finally Press Secretary Ronald Ziegler would remain in that capacity and in addition would be made an assistant to the President, taking over in that role the responsibility for what the announcement politely termed "White House communications"—actually, outright political propaganda—that was assigned during the first term to Herbert Klein, a longtime Nixon servitor and friend who had just resigned. Former Governor and Treasury Secretary John B. Connally was already aboard as a part-time, unpaid adviser concentrating on economic affairs and anti-inflation measures. Bryce N. Harlow, a Washington lobbyist who has been in and out of the White House since President Eisenhower's time and was a Nixon counsellor in 1969–70, was about to return as a senior assistant without portfolio. Here were signs aplenty of a new Nixon White House, manned at the top by experienced administrators and politicians. Ziegler and General Haig excepted, and in view of his army record Haig is not a total exception, the President would have on his controlling staff men of independent stature, in marked contrast to such assistants as Haldeman and Ehrlichman, whose sole claim to rank and power was that they had served Richard Nixon before he attained the presidency.

The recent flood of speculation about what it all means—and I'm waiting awhile before I venture judgment—omits a central point. It is that these are interim changes, mainly intended as of now to see Richard Nixon through his Watergate trouble and safely into what he hopes can be a final three years of achievement and acclaim. Melvin Laird, looking distraught and somehow embarrassed, said that he will be around for "at least a year" and made no promises beyond that. In staff discussions before Haig's military retirement was announced, the stated purpose was to keep him at the White House for a year or so. Retirement "from active duty" is not resignation. The President can recall him to active duty, still in four-star rank, at any time. General Maxwell Taylor, who retired in 1959, was recalled to duty by President John Kennedy in 1961 and made chairman of the Joint Chiefs of Staff in 1962. General Haig and Mr. Nixon are familiar with that precedent.

Ronald Ziegler's situation and future are probably of more interest to the White House press corps than to the public. But they are worth a note. The consensus of the reporters who regularly cover the White House is that Ron Ziegler is a proven deceiver and liar and that Mr. Nixon will have no credibility so long as Ziegler continues to be his chief spokesman. To the extent that this judgment is valid, it's Mr. Nixon who is the proven deceiver and liar. The President acts as if he knows it and isn't craven enough to blame his spokesman. He has declared his confidence in Ziegler and demonstrated it by giving him the added status of a full assistant. Ziegler will be around while Mr. Nixon is and while they are there it can't and won't be a believably new White House.

June 23, 1973

———

I was impressed and puzzled by the frequent quotations of the reference to Ziegler in the last paragraph of this piece that omitted the notation that "it's Mr. Nixon who is the proven deceiver and liar."

XX

Respite with Brezhnev

During the week that Richard Nixon and Leonid Brezhnev spent together in Washington and California, the visitor from Moscow had the air of a man who was doing his host a favor and the President behaved as if he agreed and was grateful for the rendered kindness. Mr. Nixon should have been grateful. This second of his meetings with Brezhnev, a consequence of and successor to the President's historic stay at the Kremlin in May of 1972, gave him and the nation a welcome though incomplete respite from the horror and threat of Watergate. Hearing the President say to the general secretary of the Soviet Communist Party on the South Lawn of the White House, on the cool and cloudy morning of June 18, that "all the world is watching us," and that "the hopes of the world rest with us," and hearing Brezhnev's translator say that he was saying that he and his companions were in America to "serve the interests of a peaceful future for all mankind," it was possible to believe and hope that Richard Nixon would surmount and survive the approaching climax of the Watergate scandals and, secured and rehabilitated in his second term, be enabled to pursue the accommodations that he had initiated with the Soviet Union and Communist China.

This was the belief and hope that Mr. Nixon relied upon, more than he could possibly rely upon the effect of his response to the Watergate disclosures already made and yet to be made, to see him through his trouble. His attempt on May 22 to cloak the illegal spying and surveillance that marked the whole pattern of Watergate mentality and behavior in the claim that he had authorized much of it for reasons of national security was in ruins. That defense had been demolished by the publication of official documents which showed beyond doubt that both the purposes and the uses of these measures were primarily political. The web of reports and testimony tying many of his closest first-term associates to the Watergate wrongs and belying any confidence that he could have been as remote from them and from the effort to conceal them as he had said he was tightened around him. Thus it was that everything the President said and did during the week of his second Soviet summit had to be and was read in part as a defense against the Watergate pressures that bore upon him. When he said at his state dinner for Brezhnev that "the question is: Shall the world's two strongest nations constantly confront each other in areas which might lead to war, or shall we work together for peace?" he was also saying to his countrymen that the question is whether the sordid Watergate affair should be allowed to bring down and drive from office a President who indeed was "working for peace" and, with his guest, aiming at a success that might "come to be measured not only in years but in decades and generations, and probably centuries."

Brezhnev proved to be an attractive and, one must assume, knowing and effective collaborator. He projected a sturdy charm in person and on television. His obvious pleasure in his first visit to the United States and in his observed encounters with the President, with senators and congressmen and with his and Mr. Nixon's guests at luncheons and state dinners imparted a certain pleasure to all who saw and met him. Just as the President had accorded first place to the general secretary and his fellows when they were in company with each other in Moscow last year, the host noticeably deferred to the guest in Washington. Even the legislators and others who formidably opposed the US trade concessions that Brezhnev sought, until and unless his government went further than it already had in removing its restrictions upon the emigration of Soviet Jews to Israel, were impressed by his arguments and evidence that the Moscow government had done more than any US administration probably would in response to another country's demands for changes in what the pressured government regarded as a matter of internal policy. Brezhnev's readiness to make the argument and present the evidence was in itself a concession from a proud and sensitive leadership that would have been unimaginable a year ago. It was a sign that General Secretary Brezhnev was also on the defensive, as anxious for his purposes as Mr. Nixon was for his purposes to justify a meeting and an approach to full accommodation that were as repellent to powerful Soviet factions as they were to vocal segments of American opinion.

The visitor and his ambassador in Washington, Anatoliy Dobrynin, must have calculated that the timing of the meeting was fortunate for them, in the sense that Mr. Nixon so clearly needed a successful outcome. But this situation and awareness played no overt part in the Nixon-Brezhnev conversations and in discussions at lower official levels. Brezhnev had said in Moscow that it would be "indecent" of him to mention Watergate or even have it in mind when he conferred with the President. Henry Kissinger and Dobrynin in Washington, and Kissinger in preparatory visits to Moscow, had worked out the script for this return summit as carefully as the scenario for Mr. Nixon's Moscow summit last year had been prepared. The dates for the Washington summit, allowing for a few days' variation either way, were set in Moscow last September. Agreements for US-Soviet cooperation in oceanography, transportation, agriculture, taxation of each country's nationals and cultural exchanges extended previous formal and informal understandings and were negotiated well in advance of the ceremonial signings in Washington, with televised fanfare and gaiety. More substantive agreements on the exchange of nuclear technology for peaceful uses, and on guidelines to govern the second phase of the US-Soviet strategic arms limitation talks, aimed at mutual and permanent restriction of each country's offensive nuclear weapons, had also been pretty well though not completely arranged beforehand. Brezhnev and his spokesman, Leonid Zamyatin, showed themselves to be acutely conscious of suspicions in the US that the huge grain sales to the Soviet Union that were negotiated last year were distinctly to Soviet advantage at American expense and that the preliminary agreement in Moscow to limit offensive nuclear armaments left the Soviets with an edge that could be dangerous if it were not curtailed and compensated for in the second round of SALT. This was why Brezhnev and Zamyatin talked about "mutually advantageous cooperation" and deplored published American notions that Mr. Nixon, in his zeal to win a peacemaker's place in history, had not only imperiled US welfare and security but had conceded more than an American president decently could to a repressive and inherently hostile Communist regime. It was sentiment of this sort that Brezhnev addressed himself to when he said at the President's dinner for him that "the reshaping of Soviet-American relations" requires much effort "to overcome the inertia of the 'cold war' and its aftereffects in international affairs, and in the minds of men."

A side effect of the Washington summit, even while it gave Mr. Nixon passing respite from Watergate, was to highlight the tensions and pressures at the Nixon White House. Right up to and through the first 48 hours of the general secretary's presence in the US, the Ervin investigating committee's plan to hear John Wesley Dean III, the President's fired and vengeful counsel, in televised testimony while Brezhnev was in conference with Mr. Nixon at the White House precipitated bitter reaction from some of the President's closest surviving associates. I heard it said that calling Dean in the summit week would be "close to treason" and would constitute proof that Senator Sam Ervin, the committee chairman, was out to "break the President and break the presidency" at any cost. At the last-minute instance of Senators Mike Mansfield and Hugh Scott, the Democratic and Republican floor leaders, Ervin and the committee put off Dean's appearance and

D. Levine 72

the damaging disclosures that he promised for a week. Mansfield
and Scott said that they acted on their own, without prodding
from the President or the White House staff. But they must have
known of the fears and feelings at the White House and have
known, too, that some of the President's men were set to attempt
to discredit the entire Watergate investigation with charges that
its conductors were willing and ready to endanger the summit and
all that it might contribute to world peace and security. As it
turned out, with the postponement granted and with Brezhnev
off to Paris and the President holed up at his California home, one
could be sure that peace and Mr. Nixon's striving for it would
figure largely in his forthcoming responses to Dean's testimony
and to the intensified pressures upon him that it is likely to gen-
erate.

One of the heralds of the defensive peace theme was Mr. Nixon's
temporary and very special adviser, John B. Connally. At his first
appearance in the White House press room since his undertaking
to assist the President for a while was announced on May 10,
Connally was asked what he thought of the summit meeting and
replied: "It's going to lay the foundations for peaceful movements
that will be of enormous benefit to the world." The implication,
which didn't need to be stated, was that any attack upon or
criticism of Mr. Nixon that impeded these peaceful movements
would be a disservice to the nation and the world. Big John's
purpose in appearing, however, had a closer connection with his
own and the President's domestic future and well-being than with
international summitry. His public shift in April from the Democratic to the Republican Party and his immediate association with
Mr. Nixon in his time of trouble had seemed to be souring on
both of them. There had been reports, believed with reason by
Washington journalists to emanate from Connally himself, that
his advice to the President on how to combat the rampant inflation and to reconstruct the recently shattered White House staff
had not been received by Mr. Nixon with the reverence and respect to which Connally had become accustomed when he was
Treasury secretary in 1971–72. He was said to be on the verge
of going home to Texas and off on a world trip that he'd been plan-

ning in early May. Such stories were not likely to enhance his value to his law clients, whom he had temporarily abandoned when the matter of conflicts of interest was raised, and who naturally regarded his standing with the President as an asset to them. Neither were the stories likely to improve his prospects of being the next Republican presidential nominee, an ambition that he disowns with moving insincerity. The day when Messrs. Nixon and Brezhnev retired to Camp David for their conclusive summit round seemed to Connally to be a good time to rebut the stories and he did so with his usual gusto. He rebutted them, that is, in a fashion that confirmed an impression that they had been true but were no longer true. With his immensely engaging smirk, he said to the assembled reporters that "y'all have some leakers that are fairly accurate." What it came to, the reporters gathered, was that he'd been in a huff and had decided to leave and had been persuaded to stick around, off and on, until midsummer. It didn't matter much, really, except that between June and midsummer the President will need all the help he can get and had evidently asked John Connally to stay with him a little longer.

June 30, 1973

XXI

Watergate Miseries

San Clemente

Near the end of the President's midsummer fortnight at what the reporters in his press party are beginning to call, with bitter humor, "our" California home, I remarked to one of the few senior assistants who accompany Mr. Nixon nowadays on his escapes from Washington that I couldn't believe that he and his advisers were about to be as stupid as current rumor had them about to be. The rumor was that the President intended to stop in Kansas City, on his way back to Washington, and appear with Clarence Kelley, the new director of the FBI, when he took his oath of office in the city where he had been chief of police. My remark troubled and puzzled the assistant. What, he asked, would be so stupid about doing that? When I said that the last thing the country, the President, Clarence Kelley and the FBI needed at this point was a ceremony that would emphasize and publicize the new director's identity with and obligation to Richard Nixon, and added that many people would see in the performance a cheap attempt by the President to shield himself from his Watergate troubles with another law-and-order pitch, the assistant said that I had it all wrong. It was right and logical and necessary, he said, that Mr. Nixon should show the country that Director Kelley was taking office with the full confidence and support of the President. The rumor was confirmed a couple of days afterward and the assistant turned to helping Mr. Nixon prepare himself for the televised display of rectitude and firmness that duly occurred.

The wounds of Watergate, and the obsessing effort of the President and the shrunken group of associates and relatives around him to persuade themselves and the public that the wounds must not, need not and will not be fatal to his presidency, have never been more apparent than during this stay in California. It should have been a happy stay, starting as it did with Leonid Brezhnev, the chairman of the Soviet Communist Party, a guest in the President's home for the final two days of their summit meeting and, toward the end, Communist China's ex-officio ambassador in Washington out for a day to confer with Mr. Nixon and Henry Kissinger. Instead it's been a miserable time, miserable for the President and for a reporter who wants his country's Presidents, including this President, to be esteemed and do well.

When Chairman Brezhnev and Mr. Nixon said their formal goodbyes on the lovely and luxuriant lawn of La Casa Pacifica, the General Services Administration was getting ready to disclose, after four years of concealment at White House orders, the federal spending of more than $700,000 for renovations, improvements and furnishings in and around the President's California home and of another $600,000 at his Florida home. The Secret Service ordered most of the work and most of it could be justified with the claim that it was necessary for security reasons. The damaging fact, however, was that the expenditures had been successively hidden and minimized since 1969. It was the prolonged concealment, rather than the expenditures themselves, that gave the business a look of shoddy chiseling and generated the reporters' cracks about "our" home on the rare occasions when we got within sight of the place.

There also was the festering and incompletely answered question of how Mr. Nixon acquired the California estate. He and his White House lawyers and spokesmen concealed for four years,

from May of 1969 to May 25, 1973, the fact that his multimillionaire friend Robert Abplanalp had made the acquisition
possible first with loans amounting to $635,000 and later by as-
suming through an otherwise undescribed "investment company"
a debt of $1.2 million so that Mr. Nixon could enjoy the privacy
and grandeur of an estate totaling 29.9 acres while actually buying
or contracting to buy 5.9 acres of it. An exaggerated newspaper report that Archibald Cox, the special Watergate prosecutor, was
preparing to investigate an undocumented and previously denied
story to the effect that 1968 Nixon campaign funds were used to
swing the original deal before Robert Abplanalp came to the rescue
drove the President into a cursing rage. He ordered his chief
spokesman, Press Secretary Ronald Ziegler, to denounce "un-
founded, malicious and scurrilous" reports and to say: "These
types of stories continue to run, the innuendo and the suggestions
continue to fly out of this environment, and it is unjust, it is unfair,
and it is not in my mind relevant to our way of life in this country
for this type of smear charge to be made against the President of
the United States . . . I would say that the President is appalled
by these consistent efforts being undertaken in the malicious—I
don't know whether you can say libelous in terms of the President—
but these constant efforts to suggest that there has been in any
way wrongdoing associated with the purchase of this property."

It was difficult for spokesmen who said that the foregoing out-
burst reflected the President's viewpoint to maintain that he was
perfectly calm and confident in his approach and reaction to his
Watergate problem. But Ziegler, his deputy Gerald Warren and
the few other White House assistants who were in occasional
touch with reporters out here did their loyal best to put about
and support an impression that Mr. Nixon is more baffled than
troubled by increasingly frequent and insistent media comment to
the effect that Watergate in all of its connotations has so impaired
his ability to govern that he ought to resign. His daughter Julie
Eisenhower said in an interview published on her 25th birthday
that last May 4, during a family discussion at Camp David, the
President posed the case for resignation and agreed with his wife
and daughters that he must stay in office for the good of the country. I judge that Daddy was told what Daddy wanted to hear and

I don't doubt the White House story that the President has never seriously contemplated resignation.

Neither I nor, to my knowledge, any other journalist is in a position to say with certainty that Mr. Nixon hasn't thought of resignation, foresees no possibility of impeachment and therefore doesn't fear it, and generally views the situation brought upon him by the Watergate scandals with full awareness of its impact and sober confidence that he will survive it. This is what we are told. One of the consequences of Watergate, capping as it does the four-year record of concealment and deception at the Nixon White House that is typified by his and his spokesmen's handling of the facts about the purchase and improvement of his homes, is that nothing we are told about his private attitudes and demeanor is inherently believable. The President himself has never been more isolated from all except his chosen intimates. The proffered stories of a more open presidency, with more and freer contact between Mr. Nixon, his Cabinet secretaries and important congressmen, are belied by evidence from his staff that he deals principally with most of its senior functionaries and with department and agency heads through his new administrative chief, General Alexander Haig. In his newly dual capacities as press secretary and assistant to the President, Ronald Ziegler is said to pass along suggestions and guidance to others at the White House. Haig passes orders. Melvin Laird, the new counsellor for domestic affairs, says that he is opening up and dispersing his own communication with domestic officialdom and its communication through him and Haig with the President. Henry Kissinger operates as he has since 1969, ascendant in foreign affairs and accountable only to the President. The purveyed impression is of a White House establishment that is warmer and looser than it was when the departed assistants, H. R. Haldeman and John Ehrlichman, ran it the way the President wanted it run. John Connally, the special and temporary adviser who appeared briefly with the President in California and then vanished for a while, got to the nub of the probable truth with something that he said at the White House on June 20. He said it in the course of arguing that Mr. Nixon's outstanding operational characteristic is "the delegation of enormous authority to other people"—the basis of the dubious claim that Mr. Nixon didn't have to know what his Watergate sinners were doing. "That is the way he operates," Connally said. "That is the way he is. I don't think you are going to change him or I am going to change him or anybody else is going to change him. You have to take him for what he is, as you do any President, because he is a human being."

Reporters who never see the President in the intimacy that Connally does have to take him for what he is said to be in private and makes himself appear to be in public. The most vivid and memorable public glimpse of him during this California stay occurred when he saw Leonid Brezhnev off at the El Toro air base near San Clemente. Brezhnev, walking with Mr. Nixon from a helicopter to the presidential plane that was to take the visitor back to Washington, veered from the planned route to chat for a moment with reporters and cameramen who were confined behind a rope. The President, glancing behind him as he walked on, saw his guest at the rope and responded to the sight in two ways, with a look at extreme irritation and by snapping to Brezhnev's interpreter, Viktor Sukhodrev, that the chairman had already said all he needed to say at the formal farewell in San Clemente. Here, in what should have been a moment of mutual pleasure and summit triumph, was an impulsive show of anger and rudeness. Brezhnev either didn't notice or pretended not to when he rejoined the President for the interrupted walk to the plane.

The available accounts of how the President reacted privately in California to Watergate developments and to printed and broadcast suggestions that he give up and resign are the kind that have to be taken on faith or rejected. My policy is to listen to them and pass them along for whatever interest they may have as examples of the image of the private Nixon that his associates wish to put abroad. Incredulous reporters are told, for instance, that the President really and truly didn't look for a single moment at his fired counsel, John Wesley Dean III, during Dean's five days of televised and immensely damaging Watergate testimony. Why not? Not because, one is told, the President was afraid to see and to hear for himself, but because he didn't need to see and hear for himself. He already knew, not necessarily all that Dean was going to say, but that it would hurt him and his cause and that's all he needed to know. Didn't he want to see and judge for himself something of how Senator Sam Ervin and the other interrogators would handle Dean? No, the answer went—he already knew that they wouldn't give "that cheap crook" the rigorous cross-examination that Mr. Nixon thought he should have got and that White House spokesmen have been saying he didn't get. When I remarked after hearing one such account that it just wasn't human, that Mr. Nixon surely wanted to and did look for a moment or two at either the live telecasts or selected snatches of the Signal Corps film record, my informant replied: "You'd watch, and I'd watch, and I did watch. But you aren't Richard Nixon and I'm not Richard Nixon. He is Richard Nixon, that's the way he is, and he is the President of the United States."

Accounts of the President's reaction to the view that he can't govern anymore and therefore should quit have him talking approximately as follows to Ronald Ziegler, General Haig and the Nixon family: "What do they mean, I can't govern? I *am* governing. When I met Pompidou in Iceland, did Pompidou say to me, sorry Mr. President, you can't govern and there's no point in talking to you? He did not. Did Brezhnev tell me that I can't govern? He did not. Are the Europeans telling Henry Kissinger that his President can't govern so there's no point in talking about our 'year of Europe?' They are not. They are talking about our 'year of Europe.' Is Congress telling me that I can't govern? It is not. It is sustaining my vetoes, isn't it? Was it telling me that I can't govern when we worked out our compromise on the Cambodia bombing? It was not. We got our extension to August 15, didn't we? So what do they mean about not governing? I can govern and I am governing and I am going to continue to govern."

Mr. Nixon spent a lot of talking time in California with Ziegler, Haig and Raymond K. Price, Jr., who has been recalled to duty as the principal speech writer after being shifted for a while to a special consultancy in the hope that he could do some leisurely and productive long-term thinking for the President. The offered accounts of what the assistants heard from the President foreshadowed a letter to Senator Ervin in which Mr. Nixon refused to testify or appear before the Watergate committee "under any circumstances" and said that the committee can't have access to presidential papers that might prove or disprove his contention that he knew nothing about the Watergate crimes when and for months after they were perpetrated. Mr. Nixon is said to have held forth to his assistants, with passion and with every sign of profound conviction, along the line that the presidency as a continuing institution would be imperiled and that their usefulness to him in his presidency would be ended if he and they had to account for and justify to outsiders the content and detail of their discussions and of other internal White House communications. In these conversations, it now appears, the President was rehearsing his letter to Senator Ervin and fortifying himself and his assistants against the interpretation that was immediately put upon it. The interpretation was that the President, while taking a probably sound and certainly defensible constitutional position, was setting himself to make known what he wants known and to withhold from Congress and the public what he doesn't want known.

An interesting and revealing aspect of the letter to Senator Ervin is the fact that the President didn't have to send and release it. The committee hadn't done anything that required it. Mr. Nixon had already said, through Ziegler, that he'd address himself once again to the Watergate matter when or soon after the current phase of the committee hearings ends. It was bound to bring down upon him the criticism and interpretation that have just been summarized. It was, I think, Richard Nixon's way of saying to the world as he has been saying to his assistants and family that he can govern and will continue to govern in his own fashion and to hell with anybody who says he can't and won't.

July 2, 1973

XXII

Truth and Tapes

A reporter who noticed that the President canceled one of his announced appointments on July 12 and postponed another one from morning to afternoon asked Deputy Press Secretary Gerald Warren whether there was any reason for the changes. Warren said later that he knew at the time that the President wasn't feeling well. But he didn't say so when he answered the question at that day's briefing for the White House press corps. He said instead that "the President has adjusted his schedule so he can spend time this morning discussing various matters with members of his staff." Several other answers and a run of routine announcements gave an impression that Mr. Nixon was, if anything, busier than usual in his West Wing office and no hint whatever that he was in fact taking it easy in his living quarters in the executive mansion, fighting off the viral pneumonia that compelled him to enter the Bethesda Naval Hospital in suburban Maryland that night. Warren said eight times, in slightly different ways, that the skeptical reporters in his audience could be sure that "the information I give you is accurate information." In a reference to the impact of the Watergate scandals on White House credibility, he also mentioned "the differences in climate that we find ourselves in now" and continued: "I think those differences make it even more vital that the information we provide you be accurate, and make us even more cognizant of our responsibilities."

It was important to the President and to Warren's immediate boss, Press Secretary Ronald Ziegler, that the reporters who regularly cover the White House be persuaded that they were getting accurate information and that the deputy press secretary was in a position to give accurate and authoritative information. It was important because Ziegler's record of evasion and deception in dealing with questions about and arising from the Watergate affair had convinced the President, as long ago as last December, that he should get himself a spokesman who would have a credibility with the working press that neither he, the President, nor Ziegler had by the end of 1972. The obvious solution would seem to have been to fire Ziegler and maybe Warren and bring in a new White House press staff. For reasons that tell a lot about Mr. Nixon, the Nixon White House and the Kafkaesque mix of circumstances and motives that make the place what it is, this was not the President's solution. He is devoted to Ziegler and, by making Ziegler an assistant to the President as well as press secretary, he has shown that he appreciates Ziegler's utter devotion to him. It is also possible that he knows that Ziegler could blow the whistle on the extent of the President's involvement in the Watergate mess and on the President's responsibility for Ziegler's endeavors to conceal any involvement there may have been. On the record to date this is only a possibility and the fact that it is noted here is just one more indicator of the corrosive suspicions that Watergate engenders. A more relevant fact is that both the President and Ziegler appear to realize that the reporters who frequent the White House press room credit Gerald Warren with an innate respect for accurate information and the obligation to provide it that they don't perceive in Ron Ziegler. Warren, aged 42, is a former journalist and a rather sedate fellow. Ziegler, aged 34, is a bouncy and (to me, anyhow) likable type who came to Mr. Nixon's service and the White House from an advertising agency. But their respective backgrounds are incidental to the main point that Warren appears to prefer the truth and Ziegler appears to fear it.

Why then didn't the President transfer Ziegler completely to other duties and designate Warren the press secretary—a course that has been recommended to him by Melvin Laird, his new counsellor for domestic affairs, and by John Connally, his temporary special adviser, among others? This is where we go straight to Kafka country. Precisely because Ziegler is totally and ineradicably identified with the Watergate deceptions, Mr. Nixon is determined that Ziegler keep the title and perform fewer and fewer of the duties of press secretary, while Warren performs more and more of them. The alternative and logical course would, in the President's clearly indicated opinion, constitute a confession of past fault on his part and a concession to his critics that he isn't prepared to make. "They will never get *that* pound of flesh," the President has said several times to Ziegler, referring to the critics. So Ziegler retains the title, makes the big announcements and enjoys a close and increasing access to the President that Warren, handling more and more of the routine briefings and gradually trying to establish himself as the regular presidential spokesman, also needs but probably never will get. Much of the long briefing session on July 12 was taken up with Warren's efforts to convince the reporters that he has the access he needs and their expressions of doubt that he either has it or, if he had it, would be permitted as Richard Nixon's spokesman to dispense the truth in matters large and small that he is inclined by nature and prior training to prefer. It's a messy solution, indeed no solution at all, to the minor portion of the President's credibility problem that a press secretary can resolve. But it's the solution chosen by Mr. Nixon and the one he's likely to stick to in the foreseeable future.

It was Ziegler, for instance, who went to the hospital with the President and, at televised briefings there, managed the medical testimony that Mr. Nixon really was ill (as he was) and not, as some people who were susceptible to the Watergate atmosphere suggested, faking illness in order to get away from Watergate troubles and pressures for a few days. Warren appeared with Treasury Secretary George Shultz at the White House when he announced the details of the President's Phase Four economic policy. Ziegler's deputy, one may be sure, will be the spokesman who usually handles the difficult questions that the new combination of tightened and relaxed controls is bound to raise and makes the best he can for the President of the evidence, if there is any, that Phase Four is at least slowing the Nixon inflation.

A White House colleague of Ziegler and Warren to whom I mentioned the Kafka atmosphere in which they all function retorted that it's really a "Kafka-Kaufman atmosphere." He was referring to George S. Kaufman, the late and zany playwright, and suggesting that the Nixon White House is shot through with intermingled tragedy, comedy and all the contradictions that beset the human condition there and elsewhere. My friend's remark was induced by the disclosure at Senator Ervin's Watergate hearings that four of Mr. Nixon's business telephones, two of his offices and the Cabinet room had been wired for secret recording of everything said on the telephones and in the bugged presidential precincts since the spring of 1971. Secret recording was not unknown in the Kennedy and Johnson times, it turned out, but nothing like or approaching the Nixon system of covert eavesdropping on a President's associates and callers had previously been attempted or heard of. The immediate and serious question was whether the President would release to the Ervin committee the recordings that in theory might prove once and for all whether he was as ignorant of the Watergate malpractices of some of his assistants and other associates as he says he was before last March 21. The indications on July 18 were that he wouldn't release the tapes, knowing though he and his White House lawyers do that his refusal to do so would be taken to be a conclusive admission of otherwise unadmitted guilt.

There are, however, a couple of secondary points about the recordings that shouldn't be overlooked. One of the points is that some of the tapes in question were played back and drawn upon by the lawyers and others who helped Mr. Nixon draft his May 22 statement of innocence, ignorance and denial. Another point is that the choice of material from these particular recordings was very selective indeed. It had to be highly selective, for the President's purposes, because the evidence on the tapes was mixed and confusing. Some of it supported the President's contentions and recollections. Some of it, often on the same tape, could be interpreted if read alone to dispute his contentions and make him out a liar. Absolute truth, I am told, is no more likely to be found in the Nixon tapes, even if they were released to the Ervin committee, than it is to be found elsewhere in the Watergate welter.

July 28, 1973

————

The disclosure in the last paragraph of the foregoing piece that Nixon assistants had drawn upon some of the Nixon tapes for his Watergate defense raised a considerable storm. It may have erred in the reference to the May 22 statement, but it was correct in first reporting that the tapes were being used and that they told a mixed story.

XXIII

A Closing Trap

Mr. Nixon said that the written statement that supplemented his televised Watergate speech on August 15 was intended "to cover the principal issues relating to my own conduct which have been raised since my statement of May 22 and thereby to place the testimony on those issues in perspective." One of the President's many difficulties with both the speech and the statement, a difficulty that contributed materially to the impression that he continued to evade the issues and conceal the truth because the truth would ruin him, was that very few really new and substantial questions about his conduct had been raised since he began on April 30 to assert the claim of innocence and ignorance that he elaborated in May and repeated in mid-August. Given so little that was new to address himself to, Mr. Nixon had very little that was new to say for himself in his third plea in four months for belief that he simply didn't know what all of those associates and assistants of his were doing to get him reelected in 1972 and therefore could not have been a party to their misdeeds. The consequent sense of futile and empty repetition of stale denials, and of equally stale attempts to take responsibility without taking blame, had much to do with the patent weakness of the Nixon performance.

It is true that the 35 witnesses and two million words of testimony and interrogation heard by Senator Sam Ervin's Watergate investigating committee before it recessed in early August added immensely to the weight of evidence and suggestion that Mr. Nixon's White House establishment and the President himself were involved in what he called, in his August 15 speech, "a whole series of acts that either represent or appear to represent an abuse of trust." It is also true, though commonly overlooked, that the President in his April and May disquisitions anticipated and dealt in some degree and fashion with all of the major questions about Watergate conduct that were raised and explored during the first phase of the Ervin hearings. He discussed and denied prior knowledge of the Watergate burglary and bugging that started it all; awareness of and participation in the prolonged effort to conceal high-level involvement in the original idiocy; any knowledge and offer on his authority of presidential clemency and hush money for the convicted Watergate defendants; prior knowledge or authorization of the felonious attempt to steal Daniel Ellsberg's psychiatric records; and any part in "illegal or improper campaign tactics." His argument that considerations of national security required and excused wiretapping and other forms of surveillance and repression, some of it still not disclosed and explained, was set forth in May and merely renewed in August.

Apart from national security, an aspect of the Watergate pattern and debate that the President largely dragged in and magnified for defensive purposes, the credibility of his assertions and positions rested upon the validity of his claim that in 1972 he departed for the first and only time in his 27 years in politics from his habit of running his own election campaigns and "to the maximum extent possible . . . sought to delegate campaign operations, to remove the day-to-day campaign operations from the President's office and from the White House." Only if it were true that he actually did this, not merely "to the maximum extent possible" but completely and inclusively, was it possible to believe that he could have been as ignorant of what was done by his lieutenants

in his behalf as he had to say he was if he was to sustain his
argument that he had to be innocent of the offenses committed
because he didn't know they were being committed. The members
and staff of the Ervin committee never seemed to grasp the central
importance of this factor in the Nixon position. There were pe-
ripheral questions about it but never during the first phase of the
hearings was there a considered and adequate effort to determine
whether the President in fact left the management of his 1972 campaign so completely to others that he truly didn't know what those
others including some of his principal White House assistants and
Cabinet associates were doing for him in his name. One of the
things they were doing for him was covering up the degree of
White House and reelection committee involvement in the Watergate burglary. As former attorney general and campaign director
John N. Mitchell testified, that exercise in concealment was deemed
until election day to be a vital campaign exercise. When Mr. Nixon
said on August 15 that "I was convinced there was no cover-up
because I was convinced that no one had anything to cover up,"
he asked the country to believe that he knew nothing whatever
about an endeavor that such intimates and senior campaign strat-
egists as Mitchell thought essential for his reelection by the huge
majority that he constantly enjoined his agents to accomplish for
him.

White House accounts of the preparation of the August 15
speech and statement suggest that the President and his principal
advisers got to a point where they didn't much care whether his
assertions of innocence bedded in ignorance were believed or not.
A consensus developed to the effect that nothing the President
could say was likely to change many opinions about him and his
guilt or innocence. What he might succeed in doing, he and his
advisers concluded, was to discredit the Watergate issue itself and
the national preoccupation with it. In a speech that in sheer mean-
ness of intent and spirit sets a high mark even for Mr. Nixon, that
is precisely what he set out to do. First we were told that the
Ervin investigation degenerated from an honest "effort to discover
the facts" to a malicious "effort to implicate the President personally." A "backward-looking obsession with Watergate" was
"causing this nation to neglect matters of far greater importance."

Major domestic legislation, important foreign policy and national security negotiations, and his ability to carry out "the mandate you gave this administration" with his reelection last year were endangered or likely to be. Therefore, the President argued, "the time has come to turn Watergate over to the courts," which was an indirect way of saying that the Ervin investigation should be terminated before it gets into such Watergate areas as the details of 1972 campaign skulduggery and the grubby solicitation and use of Nixon campaign funds. The suggestion throughout that he was the victim and target of malevolent foes rather than of a corrective search for truth, was capped with the President's call for "help to insure that those who would exploit Watergate in order to keep us from doing what we were elected to do will not succeed." It was a preposterous ploy, it was shrewdly conceived and skillfully stated, and it won't work.

It won't work because the President is in too much trouble for this or any similar ploy to halt the process of discovery and disclosure that Watergate has set in train. A measure of the extent and severity of the trouble he's in is the issue of the Nixon tapes. I leave to the contending lawyers and the judges who will decide the matter the question whether the President is constitutionally right or wrong in his view that he has an absolute power to withhold these recordings from the Ervin committee and from Special Prosecutor Archibald Cox. Two lesser points are relevant here. One of them is that a compromise solution could have been worked out with the committee and with Cox, entailing private review of the demanded tapes by a judge or by some other impartial umpire and the limited release to the committee and to the prosecutor only of the portions bearing upon the contradictions in Watergate testimony that the recordings might (or might not) resolve. Mr. Nixon rejected the compromise and deliberately sought the total confrontation now in process and on its way to the Supreme Court. The second point, supported by the President's statement that portions of the tapes at issue verify his version, is that any reasonable person must conclude from his refusal to give up the demanded tapes that he is afraid to do so. His argument that surrender of the tapes would irreparably impair his and all future presidencies by destroying the confidentiality of the White House is hogwash.

That confidentiality is invaded all the time, by voluntary and in-voluntary disclosure, and presidencies survive it. The conclusion has to be that the Nixon tapes give the lie to parts of the Nixon Watergate story.

A starker measure of the trouble the President is in is the trouble that he and Vice President Agnew are in together. The President is said at the White House to have known since last spring, and possibly since February, that a Republican prosecutor's investiga-tion of Maryland contractors' payoffs to politicians in Baltimore county, where Agnew got his political start as county executive, was going to involve some of Agnew's friends and associates and tar the Vice President by association. The President learned only when Agnew did, on or shortly before August 1, that the Vice President himself was under investigation and could be a candidate for criminal indictment. Attorney General Richardson, who had reviewed the facts and allegations accumulated by the Baltimore prosecutor and had approved a letter notifying Agnew, through one of his lawyers, that he was under investigation, gave Mr. Nixon a detailed account of the case against Agnew on the morning of August 6 and gave the Vice President the same information that afternoon. The President and the Vice President discussed the situation for an hour and 45 minutes on August 7. Agnew had a press conference on August 8, said having it was his idea, and discernibly relished the comparison of his behavior with that of the President who hadn't had a press conference and exposed himself to questions about his Watergate problems since March 15.

A strange situation developed. Agnew associates said the Presi-dent was furious with his Vice President and that their August 7 discussion was an angry encounter. Nixon associates said the Presi-dent was deeply concerned and made his concern known to Agnew, but wasn't angry with the Vice President. Mr. Nixon had a witness at the meeting, Agnew didn't. The President's witness was General Alexander Haig, White House staff chief who replaced H. R. Haldeman last May. The White House spokesman wouldn't have been saying that the Nixon-Agnew meeting was a serious but not angry discussion of a serious matter if that was not General Haig's story. Agnew people noted with bitter resentment, and the Vice President complained in public, that anonymous news sources at

the Department of Justice encouraged reports to the effect that the Vice President was in very deep trouble and in grave danger of indictment. White House officials took a similar but more cautious line in private and the President's public spokesman, Deputy Press Secretary Gerald Warren, avoided saying that Mr. Nixon was confident of his Vice President's innocence. All sorts of meanings, including a supposition that the President welcomed the Vice President's plight because it could diminish the belief of some people that the country would be better off with Agnew than Nixon in the presidency, were read into the White House attitudes. My impression is that the President understood that the case against the Vice President was serious and considered his knowledge sufficient reason to be restrained.

In one of the court briefs supporting Mr. Nixon's refusal to release his tapes to the Watergate prosecutor, the President's lawyers made occasion to say that he could not be indicted by a grand jury unless he were first impeached and removed from office. Whether a Vice President may claim the same immunity, with reasonable hope that the courts will respect the claim, is in dispute. Upon the advice of his lawyers, and with the tacit approval of Mr. Nixon's White House lawyers, the Vice President put the federal prosecutor in Baltimore on notice that he reserves the right to claim that he cannot be indicted while he is the Vice President.

September 1, 1973

————

The following account of an August 22 press conference in San Clemente was written there and appeared in *The New Republic* of September 1 as an unsigned editorial:

> The President probably made points for himself with his press conference at San Clemente on August 22. It was his first submission to questions since March 15 and since the Watergate issue heated up last spring. Although the press had been warned that the President might refuse to respond to Watergate questions, he answered 15 questions about or related to Watergate, and he made a show of doing it briskly and forthrightly. After an erratic appearance in New

Orleans, enroute to San Clemente, that caused reporters to ask a White House spokesman whether the President was "taking any medication" and whether he and his doctors thought he was "capable of performing the duties of his office" (the answers, of course, were respectively "no" and "yes"), Mr. Nixon needed to display himself on national television in good form, in visible command of himself and his situation, and in this he succeeded on the 22nd.

Some of the answers, however, left us with that familiar and uneasy feeling about Richard Nixon. There was, for instance, his reference to the secret meeting that he and his departed assistant, John Ehrlichman, had with Judge Matthew Byrne of Los Angeles at the western White House when Judge Byrne was conducting the trial of Daniel Ellsberg and the President was looking for an FBI director to replace Patrick Gray. Because the Ellsberg trial wasn't discussed, Mr. Nixon saw nothing wrong with the meeting and with the suggestion to Judge Byrne that he might be offered the FBI directorship after the trial was over. Can the President, a lawyer, actually be that oblivious to such obvious impropriety? The answer, his answer, is that he can be and is.

Mr. Nixon distorted the thrust of a recent Supreme Court decision bearing upon the extent of his inherent powers. He gave a deceptive impression that his former assistant, H. R. Haldeman, had had less access to the Nixon White House tapes than he actually had. He suggested that his failure to ask people who could have told him about Watergate behavior when it was occurring last year was the fault of the people he didn't ask. But our favorite answer, favored because it tells so much about Mr. Nixon, occurred when he was asked whom he had in mind when he referred in his Watergate speech of August 15 to "those who would exploit Watergate" in order to impede and wreck his presidency. After remarking rather hastily that "where the shoe fits, people should wear it," he got to the nub of his thinking on the subject: ". . . What I am saying is this: people who do not accept the mandate of 1972, who do not want the strong America that I want to build, who do not want the foreign leadership that I want to give, who do not want to cut down the size of this government bureaucracy . . . people who do not want these things naturally would exploit any issue—if it weren't Watergate, anything else—in order to keep the President from doing his job . . . I think they would prefer that I fail."

It would appear that good-faith opposition and criticism have ceased to exist for Mr. Nixon. There's a word for the state of mind that he reveals. The word is paranoia.

XXIV

Out in the Open

San Clemente

Since the President was last reported upon in this space, he has made a televised spectacle of himself in New Orleans. He has confounded and defeated his media adversaries at a news conference in San Clemente. He has asked the Senate to let him replace Secretary of State William Rogers with Henry Kissinger. He has submitted to the humiliating necessity of presenting evidence, in the form of an auditing firm's report, that there was nothing crooked in the purchase of his San Clemente estate. And, in a way so petty that the merest mention of it is embarrassing, he has let his hatred of the press take him beyond the bounds of rationality.

My folly in choosing to fly directly from Washington to California instead of accompanying the President's press party to New Orleans debars any pretense at firsthand appraisal of his performance there. I must rely upon the accounts of other reporters, television film, and an excellent recording of Mr. Nixon's speech to the Veterans of Foreign Wars. There was every reason for the President to be at his best in New Orleans. He had just had two presumably restful days at his Florida home. His principal subject was to be his Indochina policy, and his VFW audience was sure to be receptive to anything he had to say about that. Local police and Secret Service reports of a conspiracy to kill the President—a plot that faded into the mist of rumor once he had come and gone—caused a change in his motorcade route that was said to disappoint and annoy him. But his spokesmen hardly mentioned this when they were later asked to explain his heard and witnessed behavior. When he saw reporters and cameramen closer to him than he wanted or had expected them to be, he lunged at Press Secretary Ronald Ziegler and snarled at him and shoved him. During his VFW speech, the President slurred a distressing number of his words. Reporters who have been observing him for years thought they saw something indefinably but unmistakably odd in his gait and his gestures. Some of them thought that he was drunk. None of them, so far as I know, was sure enough of that impression to report or even suggest it in published and broadcast accounts. Because the impression was so much a feature in the remembered scene, I report it without apology. I also accept the assertions of Nixon assistants that the President does not drink at midday, certainly not before he is to make a public address, and drinks very little at any time. The official explanation, in part implied and in part explicit, that Mr. Nixon in New Orleans showed and succumbed to the strain that he's been under for many months, what with the Watergate scandals and other troubles and pressures, seems sufficient and believable to me. It should be added that a senior Nixon assistant who was with the President in New Orleans and who later saw a televised replay of the VFW appearance and speech was shocked and disbelieving when he was told of the impression reported here. This assistant thought and told Mr. Nixon that he'd done extremely well in New Orleans. I gather that the President didn't quarrel with this estimate of the performance, though some of his other assistants did. They encouraged a later report that the President held a promised press conference in California sooner than he'd first intended because he agreed with advisers who felt that the impact of the New Orleans spectacle could be disastrous and had to be quickly offset.

There was no corresponding dispute at the western White House about the impact of Mr. Nixon's San Clemente press conference. His people judged it to be an unqualified triumph. I suspect that their judgment of it was better than that of the reporters, myself among them, who tended to mull over the many evasions and equivocations in the President's answers to the Watergate questions that were put to him and to minimize the effect that his readiness to respond to the questions appears to have had. There's a certain euphoria, and no doubt a good deal of wishful self-deception, in the expressed conviction that the President has put the worst of his Watergate travail behind him. How he and trusted White House assistants can really believe this, given the prospect of Watergate indictments and looming confrontations with the courts and Congress over his power to withhold evidence, baffles me. But the attested and reportable fact is that the President and his assistants do believe it.

In due course, no doubt, I shall work up the proper reverence for Henry Kissinger's imminent duality as secretary of State and assistant to the President for national security affairs. It is a development of considerable importance; it probably bodes well for the conduct of foreign policy in the remaining Nixon years; and it is quite possible that Kissinger will prove to be a splendid secretary of State. Right now, however, I can only marvel at the sequence of events that preceded the President's announcement at his San Clemente press conference on August 22 that Secretary Rogers' resignation had been accepted and that Kissinger would be nominated to succeed him. The possibility that he might become secretary of State and retain his White House job dawned upon Kissinger last May or thereabouts. Very soon thereafter it became apparent to his assistants on the National Security Council staff that he wanted and expected this to happen and that his frequent protestations to the contrary were so much balderdash. In mid-July Kissinger began discussing with some of his assistants the prospect that they might be transferred from the NSC staff to the State Department in order to help him master its massive and formidable bureaucracy. Rogers, a friend of the President's since the 1940s and the last of Mr. Nixon's original Cabinet appointees, evinced a rather puzzling reluctance to resign from a position that he'd been saying since 1969 he wanted to hold only through the first Nixon term. The secretary's reluctance to leave it in 1973 was puzzling because he had been in Kissinger's shadow from the start of their respective tenures and had garnered far more humiliation than honor. On August 16 Rogers spent some 90 minutes with the President at the White House. Kissinger's NSC associates noticed after the meeting that he perked up and appeared to be more assured than he'd lately been. Rogers dated his letter of resignation the 16th. At a press conference on the 20th, the date of the President's letter of acceptance and professed regret, Rogers spoke of coming foreign affairs developments as if he expected to be at the department indefinitely. Departing Cabinet officers usually make their resignations effective when their successors are confirmed by the Senate. In the tart and cryptic first sentence of an otherwise warm and friendly letter to the President, Rogers made his resignation effective September 3.

Since the National Security Council and the post of assistant for national security affairs were created by law in 1947, nobody has simultaneously been secretary of State and the President's chief staff adviser on foreign policy. Some of Kissinger's subordinates on the NSC staff are saying that he can't spend the time at the Department of State that the secretaryship normally requires and be the President's man in the sense and to the extent that the assisant for national security affairs is expected to be. It's being said at the State Department that he can't spend the time at the White House and accord his role there the priority that it normally requires and be an effective secretary of State. Although other and perhaps more serious conflicts of duty and interest are built into the complex system of interdepartmental groups and committees that Kissinger has dominated from the White House, my guess is that he will surmount the difficulties and anomalies and surprise a lot of people, possibly including himself, by making the dual role workable and effective. It's clear that he, a Jew born in Germany and the first secretary of State with that background, profoundly wants and hopes to be applauded and remembered as a great and creative secretary. Here's wishing him well.

The President's property audit climaxed a prolonged study in the penalties of avoidable deceit. From July of 1969 to May 25, 1973, he concealed the essentially innocent though rather embarrassing fact that his multimillionaire friend Robert Abplanalp had made the purchase of the Nixon estate in San Clemente possible with a series of loans and land acquisitions under cover of a blind trust. From last May 25, when the Abplanalp assistance was incompletely revealed, until August 27, Mr. Nixon brought further suspicion and recrimination upon himself by hiding the fact that another rich friend and frequent benefactor, Charles G. (Bebe) Rebozo, was a partner in the San Clemente land deal until Abplanalp bought out his interest shortly before the audit was published. The main purpose of the audit was to demonstrate that 1968 Republican campaign funds in the custody of the President's sometime attorney Herbert Kalmbach didn't have to be used and were not used to finance the original San Clemente purchase. Kalmbach, who is deeply involved in Watergate doings, swore in a civil deposition in July that campaign money wasn't used for the purchase. A sufficient commentary upon the sorry business is that the President still felt it necessary to prove that he hadn't lied when he said through a White House spokesman that he had not used party funds to buy his California home.

Mr. Nixon's latest display of contempt and dislike for the press wouldn't be worth mentioning if it didn't also entail a characteristic exercise in White House stupidity. On its face it was a matter of refusing to let the traveling press, principally the AP and UPI correspondents, know when the President sallies forth from his residence and office compound at the western White House for motor rides and visits to nearby beaches or restaurants. Even Presidents are entitled to some privacy now and then, and the whole thing would not matter if it had not required Deputy Press Secretary Gerald Warren, who has been trying for months at the President's instruction to establish his credibility as the functioning White House spokesman, to confess that even he was denied prompt and accurate information about the President's movements. It struck Warren's audience in the California press room as a needless and futile exercise in concealment.

September 8, 1973

XXV

Shades of Meaning

If the members and staff of the Senate Watergate committee were smarter than they have been up to now, they would be preparing to make the President sorry that, at his August 22 press conference in San Clemente, he mentioned Clark MacGregor and thereby drew attention to a deposition that MacGregor gave under oath in a civil suit last July 20. MacGregor was the second and last director of Mr. Nixon's Committee for the Re-election of the President. With notable speed and foresight he resigned from that job on November 8, the day after the 1972 election, and became the United Aircraft Corporation's chief lobbyist in Washington. Before he replaced former Attorney General John Mitchell as the reelection committee's director, 14 days after the Watergate burglar-buggers were caught at the Democratic National Committee head-quarters in Washington, MacGregor was in turn a Republican congressman from Minnesota, a defeated candidate for the Senate in 1970, and a White House counsellor in charge of Mr. Nixon's congressional relations.

The last thing MacGregor would want to do, one presumes, would be to embarrass Mr. Nixon or add the merest whit to the evidence that the President has been less than truthful in his pleas that he knew nothing about the campaign misdeeds now connoted by "Watergate" when they were perpetrated and, until very late in the game, nothing about the effort at the White House and the reelection committee to conceal and minimize high-level participation in and responsibility for them. But this is what MacGregor did in his deposition. His account of a conversation that he had with the President on June 30 of last year, when Mr. Nixon asked him to replace Mitchell at the reelection committee, differs to the point of contradiction with the President's statement at San Clemente that MacGregor undertook on that occasion to "conduct a thorough investigation" of "his entire committee staff" and any involvement of its members in the Watergate affair. More generally and more importantly, insofar as the viability of the President's basic claim of ignorance and consequent innocence is concerned, MacGregor's sworn account of his relationship with Mr. Nixon during the campaign is substantially inconsistent with two Nixon statements. The President said on April 30 that "to the maximum extent possible . . . I sought to delegate campaign operations, to remove the day-to-day campaign decisions from the President's office and from the White House." On August 22, in the course of deploring Watergate for the umpteenth time, Mr. Nixon said that "had I been running the campaign rather than trying to run the country and particularly the foreign policy of this country at this time, it would never have happened."

Exact though repetitious quotation of a part of the President's reference to MacGregor at San Clemente is necessary if the full contrast between the two accounts is to be conveyed. Mr. Nixon was asked if he could "tell us who you personally talked to in directing that investigations be made both in June of '72 . . . and last March 21." The relevant portion of his reply began: "Certainly. In June I, of course, talked to Mr. MacGregor first of all . . . He told me that he would conduct a thorough investigation as far as his entire committee staff was concerned. Apparently that investigation was very effective except for Mr. Magruder"—and here the President said that "Mr. MacGregor does not have to assume responsibility" for believing the lies that the committee's deputy director, Jeb Stuart Magruder, was telling at the time.

MacGregor said in his civil deposition that he met with the President in his Oval Office "at or shortly before 5 P.M. on Friday, June 30," and indicated that they were together well over an hour. "Most of the time," MacGregor said, "he and I spent talking about his hopes and dreams for a second term and what he hoped to accomplish." One of the interrogating lawyers asked MacGregor: "In the course of your conversation with the President, did he mention the Watergate affair. . . ?" MacGregor answered: "It was discussed briefly by us. I said . . . that I was familiar with the fact that it had been asserted by several people, both at the White House and at the Committee for the Re-election of the President, that no person in a position of authority or responsibility had any foreknowledge of or involvement in the Watergate and I indicated that I was assuming that I could rely on that and he said, 'I believe you can,' or words to that effect." MacGregor swore that during his first days with the committee he told John Mitchell and others, in effect: "I am taking the position with the understanding that nobody who is holding over from the Mitchell era had any knowledge of or any involvement in . . . the Watergate." He also said that he made some inquiries of staff members, rather casual inquiries by his description, in order to be able to say at press conferences that he "had been given personal assurance" that nobody "in a position of authority or responsibility" was involved. By that time the official view was that G. Gordon Liddy, the affiliated finance committee's counsel, was not "in a position of authority or responsibility" and, later on, that his indictment and conviction therefore had no significance. Fred Malek, a White House assistant who soon joined MacGregor and Magruder at the reelection committee as a second deputy director, swore in a similar civil deposition last July 4 that he and MacGregor accepted John Mitchell's finding and report that there was no high-level involvement. Malek then said under oath: "We made a conscious decision not to seek information on it." So much, in sum, for Mr. Nixon's assertion at San Clemente that MacGregor "told me that he would conduct a thorough investigation" and that "that investigation was very effective."

H. R. Haldeman, then the President's chief administrator and for practical purposes his deputy in management of the 1972 campaign, figured importantly in MacGregor's description of the relationship between him as the committee director and the President. MacGregor summarized Mr. Nixon's instructions to both of them on June 30 as follows: "One, that I would take direction in the conduct of the campaign from and after July 3 from the President and the President only" and "when either I was traveling or he was traveling and we might have difficulty in reaching each other personally, that Bob Haldeman would be the channel of communication between the President and me." MacGregor quoted the President as saying: "Clark, as you know, everybody has suggestions, particularly those who have been associated with me in past campaigns, as you have. I will be offering suggestions to you and making recommendations. I know that you will weigh them as you have [in the past], but you make the decision. If you want to consult with me about any decisions you may make, let me know directly or communicate it through Haldeman." MacGregor said that both the President and Haldeman indicated that they were pleased with the way he operated, "so that there was very little direction or instruction" from the White House. He indicated that his fairly frequent meetings with the President dealt mostly with the President's "personal campaign," rather than with the overall effort. But he also said that Mitchell when he was the committee director, and MacGregor after he succeeded Mitchell, regularly attended Haldeman's senior staff meetings at the White House each morning and that campaign matters were discussed. All in all MacGregor's total account just didn't square with Mr. Nixon's contention that he effectively removed campaign operations and decisions "from the President's office *and from the White House.*"

MacGregor's account squared much better with one that Jeb Magruder gave at a Harvard seminar in January 1973, when he was in trouble but not yet indicted and not dreaming that he'd soon be pleading guilty to perjurious obstruction of justice. Harvard University Press has published an edited transcript of the seminar discussions (*Campaign '72—The Managers Speak*) and in it Magruder says: "There was basically a triad of decision-makers—the President, Bob Haldeman and John Mitchell—until July of '72. They were in constant consultation with each other

over major activities. . . . We agreed that the Committee to Reelect would . . . stay out of the policy decision-making process
. . . Similarly, the White House stayed out of the political organizational process . . . We [at the committee] used the same staff
system that is used at the White House. We broke up the campaign initially into 16 groups and had deadlines as to when we
had to have decisions made; we put the decision papers together
and fired them off through John Mitchell into Bob Haldeman and
the President . . . When Clark MacGregor came over [to the
committee] in '72, we remained exactly in the same posture and
continued along in exactly the same process that we had started
back in May of '71. . . . I don't think it was a mystery."

It wasn't a mystery, except to the extent that the President and
his principal political advisers contrived a protective mystery with
their associated reelection and finance committees. Such words as
"lies" and "liar" are too easily thrown about in this corrupted time,
on regretted occasion by me, and it is not contended here that
MacGregor and Magruder make an outright liar of Mr. Nixon.
Differences of interested recollection don't have to be dishonorable
differences. Shades of meaning flicker over the Watergate scene
and defy precise judgment. With this allowed, however, the kindest
possible judgment has to be that Mr. Nixon really ought to watch
his words and respect the facts with more care than he frequently
does.

At a televised press conference in Washington on September 5,
the President's second in two weeks after five months of hiding
from Watergate questions, Mr. Nixon demonstrably departed from
fact—in this instance, his own previous version—only once. He
answered "nothing whatever" when he was asked whether anything in the White House tapes that he is withholding from Senate
investigators and the courts would "reflect unfavorably on your
Watergate position." He seemed to have forgotten that he had
said in a letter to Senator Sam Ervin last July 23 both that "the
tapes are entirely consistent with . . . what I have stated to be
the truth" and that "they contain comments that persons with different perspectives and motivations would inevitably interpret in
different ways." The President's evident purpose was to further
the notion that snide journalists, leering and sneering television

commentators and a hostile and dilatory Congress were frustrating his effort to get away from scandal and on with "the business of the people." He had a point and he made it well.

September 15, 1973

———

Not surprisingly, the Ervin committee failed once again to get at the very basis of Mr. Nixon's Watergate position—that he let others foul up his 1972 campaign—when it finally got around to questioning MacGregor several weeks after the foregoing appeared.

XXVI

Back to Work

A sign that the President is recovering from the worst of Watergate's personal effects upon him was the ready admission at his press conference on September 5 that public confidence in him has been "worn away" and that restoring eroded confidence is a problem. True enough, the admission came with a whine. Mr. Nixon suggested that nightly "leers" and "sneers" of television commentators dealing in leaked rumor and innuendo, rather than the cascade of proven and indicated wrong that constitutes Watergate, had caused the loss of confidence. But he didn't blink at the fact of lost confidence and he edged closer than he previously had to acknowledging that he himself had lately been through and survived some extremely low moments when he said: "Now, how is it restored? Well, it is restored by the President not allowing his own confidence to be destroyed; that is to begin. And, second, it is restored by doing something." He invited the media and the country to turn their attention from "the more fascinating area of Watergate"—that whine again—to his foreign and domestic initiatives and said that when this happens "the people will be concerned

about what the President does, and I think that that will restore
the confidence." With a leer and sneer of his own at the journalists
in his presence, but also with a healthy note of self-awareness, he
concluded: "What the President says will not restore it, and what
you ladies and gentlemen say will certainly not restore it."

The low level of confidence in Mr. Nixon that prevails among
the reporters who regularly attend his doings and goings predates
Watergate and is a poor measure of his current problems. But the
reaction in that company of professional doubters to the announcement that he was returning from San Clemente to smog-smitten
Washington on the Friday before Labor Day, instead of passing
the holiday weekend on the pleasant California coast, did indicate
the difficulty that the President and his spokesmen have in getting
themselves believed even when they deserve belief. Nothing that the
spokesmen said dispelled a suspicion that some hidden crisis,
the favorite supposition being that it was connected with Vice
President Agnew and a two-hour talk that he and Mr. Nixon had
in total privacy the day after the President returned, called Mr.
Nixon from San Clemente sooner than he'd intended. Maybe it
did, but the available evidence was to the contrary. Press Secretary
Ronald Ziegler said on the evening of the President's arrival at
San Clemente that he probably wouldn't stay over Labor Day.
After his August 22 press conference at San Clemente, an event
that the President and his assistants rated a success for him, the
word passed that he was preparing in California for an early and
aggressive show of activity—"doing something"—in Washington
and elsewhere. Alexander Haig, the new chief of the President's
staff, said several days before the early return was confirmed that
Mr. Nixon would be going back sooner than the reporters had expected in order to "recharge his body-clock"—meaning, adjust to
the three-hour time difference between Washington and California
—before undertaking a heavy Washington schedule.

This explanation could have been taken as a confession, presumably unwitting, that the President has come to be more vulnerable to the strains of travel across continental time zones than he's
seemed to be in the past. Reporters who normally are avid for any
hint that Mr. Nixon has fallen below par, physically or mentally,

didn't grab at General Haig's body-clock metaphor in that way. They laughed at it, bandying it about among themselves as one more example of the silly stuff and talk that emanates from the upper reaches of the Nixon White House. They were so intrigued with this sort of jibe, in fact, that they generally overlooked what may have been an interesting coincidence. In the course of trying to dampen speculation that a sudden call from Vice President Agnew for urgent consultation about his troubles with a federal grand jury investigation in Maryland, and about the possibility of his being indicted, was pulling the President back to Washington, Nixon assistants said that Agnew's request for a meeting with the President was received on Tuesday, August 28, and that the Vice President indicated then that he was in no particular hurry. Some of the same Nixon assistants thought for a while on that same Tuesday morning that the President was returning to Washington that day and rearranged their own plans on the assumption that he was. The urgency passed, if there was any, and the President returned on the evening of August 31, with a pack of disbelieving and disgruntled journalists in his wake.

Some insight into the way the President is going about "doing something" is provided by the preliminaries to his September 5 press conference. Despite all the talk from his staff about a newly open White House—and despite considerable effort in California to open the senior White House staff to reporters—the President is dealing now with fewer people than he did in the heyday of departed Bob Haldeman and John Ehrlichman. If such be possible, he is more secretive now than he was then. Some of the few assistants who work closely with him and see him regularly plead, when asked for some clue to how Mr. Nixon really feels about Watergate or the Agnew problem or anything else, for understanding that they don't know because he doesn't tell even them. "He doesn't confide, really confide, in *anybody*," one of these assistants said the other day. Only three assistants—General Haig, Ziegler and Patrick Buchanan—were consulted in any material way during the discussions of when and whether to follow up the August 22 press conference with another one in Washington. The President said in California that he intended to have more press conferences. But he wouldn't say when he'd have the next one. He appears to have been genuinely undecided, torn between ever-deepening dislike for the media and awareness that he generally does well for himself in his encounters with reporters. It was not until late afternoon of Tuesday, September 4, that he finally told Ziegler and Buchanan that he'd have a press conference at 3 P.M. the next day and authorized Ziegler to stage it as a fully televised extravaganza in the White House East Room. Deputy Press Secretary Gerald Warren, who has replaced Ziegler as the President's daily spokesman, was told of the decision at the last possible moment on the Wednesday morning, just before he was to brief the White House press corps. Raymond Price, one of the President's principal idea men and writers, and Ken Clawson, a press assistant who is doing what he can to open up the White House to reporters, never were told officially that there was going to be a news conference that day. They heard about it from reporters. Afterward Pat Buchanan had a task of a kind that he seldom enjoys. In print and on the air the press conference was widely judged to have been a great success for Mr. Nixon, and Buchanan compiled and digested for the President a stack of transcripts and reports to that effect.

What the President means by "doing something" was memorably illustrated at the White House the next day. He had said at the press conference that he found the record of Congress this year "very disappointing" and suggested that its omissions and mistakes, in matters ranging from cuts in his defense budget to neglect of Nixon measures to develop additional energy sources, could destroy any chances of negotiating strategic arms restraints and reductions with the Soviet Union, bring on acute fuel shortages in the next and succeeding winters, and place the country at the mercy of rapacious Arab oil suppliers. At their weekly appearance in the White House press room, his Republican floor leaders, Senator Hugh Scott and Representative Gerald Ford, discovered in the President's remarks "a note of conciliation and cooperation" that the media had failed to discern and report and Mr. Nixon, in subsequent statements, professed to have an affection and respect for Congress that somehow hadn't emerged from his press conference. In vetoing a bill that would have increased the federal minimum wage from $1.60 to $2.20 an hour by next July

1, the President offered to cooperate with Congress in devising "a moderate and balanced set of amendments" that would accomplish comparable increases in the minimum over the next three years and, in his view, protect instead of imperil "employment opportunities for low wage earners and the unemployed." At midafternoon he called photographers and reporters into his office for a picture session with Treasury Secretary George Shultz, who was about to go abroad for a series of trade and monetary negotiations. The President's purpose was to do the little he could about a horrendous jump in the wholesale price index that was to be announced the following day. Shultz was loaded with figures indicating that soybean, hog, corn and some other raw food prices that had contributed to the increase had fallen drastically since the index statistics were collected in mid-August. Mr. Nixon seemed to some of the few reporters who were hanging around the White House press room at the time to be a bit jumpy himself. His talk raced from taxes to inflation to his pending foreign trade bill and the unhappy fact that its prime mover in Congress, Chairman Wilbur Mills of the House Ways and Means Committee, was recuperating in a hospital from a back operation. Mr. Nixon got off one of those flighty disconnected oral passages that don't signify anything but are irresistibly quotable: "Wilbur Mills' incapacity—I don't know if an operation, a disc operation, which if he had asked me, I would have told him never to have had one—I haven't had one, but I have never known one to be successful. The surgeons always want to cut."

The President addressed himself in the next few days to the nation's looming problems with energy sources; to the sheaf of domestic measures, some of them dating back to 1970–71, that he has recommended and Congress has neglected or shelved; and, with more enthusiasm then he has evinced for a good many of the languishing legislative recommendations, to revised versions of the law-and-order themes that served him well in 1968 and 1972. The object of the activity was to show that he was indeed "doing something" and most of it probably helped, as the President had said he intended it to help, in restoring the confidence in him and his presidency that had "worn away." There remain an unchecked inflation and the prospects of more indictments and criminal trials of former staff and Cabinet associates and, it could be, of the Vice President. Special Prosecutor Archibald Cox, arguing to appellate judges that the President must not be allowed to withhold tape recordings of Nixon conversations from a grand jury looking into the Watergate scandals, said that the hidden evidence could have to do with criminal conduct and conversation involving the President. So the specter is still there. Getting back to work and "doing something" may obscure the specter for a while but it won't go away.

September 22, 1973

XXVII

Agnew's Case

At this writing on September 19, it's been 50 days since the United States attorney who conducts federal prosecutions in Maryland notified Vice President Agnew that he is being investigated and may be indicted on charges that he has violated laws "including but not limited" to statutes having to do with conspiracy, extortion, bribery and income taxes. US Attorney George Beall's letter of August 1 to one of the Vice President's lawyers remains the only formal and privileged basis for continuing news reports that the Vice President is accused of criminal acts. These reports have it that he is accused of taking payoffs from contractors who did business with Baltimore County and the state of Maryland when Mr. Agnew was, in turn, the county's chief administrator and governor of Maryland, and that he accepted improper payments from some of the same benefactors after he became Vice President in 1969.

President Nixon, the Vice President and Attorney General Elliot Richardson have referred in various contexts and ways to the fact that Mr. Agnew is under criminal investigation. But no accuser has come forward and said publicly, in his or her own name, that the Vice President has committed any crime or done anything wrong. Although the prosecutor's letter mentioned "allegations concerning possible violations" and warned the Vice President that any records and information that he voluntarily provided "could be used against him in a criminal case," the US attorney made no charges of his own in the letter and made none in the following 50 days. In this period no warrant was issued. No indictment was sought, and no evidence concerning the Vice President was presented to a grand jury that has been sitting intermittently in Baltimore and looking into charges of corruption in the award of state and county contracts. Yet the regular publication of new allegations, the elaboration of old ones, and the ways in which the Vice President, the President, the Agnew staff, the White House staff and the Justice Department dealt with the matter profoundly affected the Vice President, the Nixon presidency and the Agnew-Nixon relationship. A report that Agnew was about to resign and an initial indication at the White House that the President would be neither displeased nor astonished if he did brought Mr. Nixon to the sad pass of having a spokesman say for him: "I am denying that there is any truth to stories that there is a disposition on the part of the White House or people in the White House to force the Vice President to resign or that the White House is applying pressure on the Vice President to resign."

Many of the reports that stimulated this situation and kept it alive were attributed to "sources close to the investigation" and often simply to "sources" that were not identified or characterized at all. But the sources were good enough for the *Wall Street Journal, New York Times, Washington Post,* Knight Newspapers, *Time* and *Newsweek* among other publications digging for the story. The most pointed and damaging of the reports had three Maryland engineers and contract consultants who were longtime friends, supporters and associates of the Vice President trying to save their skins by tattling on him to the prosecutor. More recent reports, less serious but suggesting a long run of tawdry behavior, had the Vice President accepting $15,000 from a retired Mary-

land industrialist who seemingly had nothing to gain from Agnew; free food for the family larder from the vice president of a supermarket chain; and a large "celebrity discount" on the rental of a luxury hotel apartment that the Agnews occupied until recently.

Attorney General Richardson, responding by letter to the Vice President's complaint that Justice Department officials were leaking some of the reports to the press, reminded him that "a considerable number of people in and out of government are aware of some details of the investigation. Its outlines are known to a number of witnesses, individuals under investigation, their lawyers, select members of my, your, and the White House staff, and certain investigative personnel of the Internal Revenue Service." The effect of this observation, and of much else said at the White House and the Justice Department, was to sustain and strengthen an impression that a serious investigation of serious charges had placed the Vice President in a very serious situation.

Why the President and the attorney general thus contributed to an impression that could not possibly do the Nixon administration any good puzzled many journalists and others following the affair. My impression is that there is no great cause for puzzlement. The sequence of known events suggests that the President and the attorney general have been aware since late July that the Vice President's situation is indeed serious and that they have had no choice except to handle the resultant problem with the maximum restraint permitted by so grave a situation and prospect. The attorney general would not have permitted prosecutor Beall to send the August 1 notice to an Agnew attorney if he had not been convinced after a review of the evidence then in hand that a grave warning to the Vice President was not only justified but necessary. Nor would Mr. Richardson have said later, as he has said and was still saying after the 50 days, that he must decide and had yet to decide whether the evidence against the Vice President justified a request for indictment and, if it did, whether an incumbent Vice President is subject to the criminal process or must first be impeached and removed from office. This last is the position taken and asserted by the President's White House lawyers, on Mr. Nixon's behalf, in connection with the Watergate scandals, and the Vice President has indicated to the Baltimore prosecutor that he may claim the same immunity from criminal prosecution so long as he holds the office. A reference to the attorney general in the White House spokesman's previously quoted denial of a "disposition" to force the Vice President to resign suggests that Mr. Nixon's final attitude toward the Vice President and his continued incumbency will turn upon Elliot Richardson's finding that the case against Spiro Agnew does or does not call for either indictment or impeachment. The spokesman, Deputy Press Secretary Gerald Warren, indicated that he was trying to say precisely what the President had told him to say. He explained his earlier refusal to comment in any way upon a report that the Vice President was discussing and considering immediate resignation—a reaction that left the impression that the President wouldn't mind or be surprised if Agnew quit—by arguing that any White House comment would be "inappropriate" while the attorney general was assessing the case against the Vice President. The President's spokesman added: "I will not have any further comment until the attorney general completes his assessment of this situation and addresses it." There could hardly have been a clearer indication that the President is waiting "until the attorney general completes his assessment" and, at the least, expects the Vice President to await and act upon the same assessment.

The assumption at the White House is that the President must have considered and be considering alternatives to Agnew in the vice presidency. How his thinking and preferences run in this regard, I don't know and I doubt that any of his assistants know. But the subject can't be discussed at this point without reference to former governor, Treasury secretary and special adviser John B. Connally. He is one of Mr. Nixon's favorite characters; he organized and led Democrats for Nixon last year; he quit the Democratic Party and turned Republican early this year; and he's currently running about the land, testing his appeal to Republicans and to the general electorate, with a view toward going after the Republican nomination for President in 1976. Mr. Nixon had his friend Connally at the White House for a little talk the other day and had it announced afterward that Connally may be traveling abroad, to Europe and the Middle East, on presidential business in the vaguely defined future. Mr. Nixon teased Agnew and Agnewites early last year with indications that he might prefer Connally to Agnew on the 1972 ticket. Given a vacancy in the vice presidency this year, the President will have to nominate a successor, subject to approval by House and Senate majorities. Connally? It could be. For better or for worse, we'll soon know whether a successor is required and, if so, who it will be.

September 29, 1973

XXVIII

Inquest for Agnew

Spokesmen for both the President and the Vice President emphasize the fact that Mr. Agnew requested his meetings with Mr. Nixon on August 7, September 1 and September 20, and that the President initiated a fourth and, up to then, climactic discussion with the Vice President at the White House on September 25. Before the President and the Vice President met alone on the 25th, Attorney General Elliot Richardson and Assistant Attorney General Henry Petersen, who directs criminal proceedings at the Department of Justice, gave Mr. Nixon what he called "an assessment of the situation." The unprecedented situation that they assessed for the President resulted from the federal investigation of reports —not as yet formal charges, although the President and the Vice President were soon calling them charges—that Spiro Agnew extorted and accepted bribes from contractors when he was a county official and governor of Maryland and took thousands of dollars from some of the same sources after he became Vice President.

Nearly all that is known at this writing of what passed between the President and the Vice President and of the situation that they and the country confront is set forth in statements by the attorney general and the President; a letter from the Vice President to Speaker Carl Albert of the House of Representatives; sparse accounts of the Nixon-Agnew meeting offered by the President's spokesman, Deputy Press Secretary Gerald Warren; and a brief, oral denial by the Vice President that the possibility of his resigning was discussed by him and the President. Here, derived entirely from the official and published evidence, is my reading of what Mr. Nixon was calling "the situation" as it stood on September 27.

It is all too clear that Richardson, Petersen and George Beall, the US attorney conducting the Maryland investigations and prosecutions of bribery in public business, are convinced that the evidence involving Vice President Agnew is substantial and damning. The events on and after the 25th confirmed, if any confirmation were needed, prior indications that the President, the Vice President and the attorney general have known since last July and possibly for quite a while longer that Mr. Agnew was in a kind and degree of trouble that, sooner or later, was bound to bring into question the feasibility and propriety of his continuance in office. The President's spokesman, the Vice President's spokesman, and Mr. Agnew himself have denied that his resignation was requested, offered or discussed at his first three meetings with Mr. Nixon on this matter. After the fourth meeting the President's spokesman said again that the Vice President's resignation was neither requested nor offered. He was extremely reluctant to say whether it was discussed. Derisive reporters drove the spokesman to say that resignation "would have been among the options discussed" and, finally and flatly, that "it was" among the options discussed. His way of saying this did not indicate to me that he intended to acknowledge that it was discussed as a serious or desired possibility. But some reporters interpreted the spokesman's grudging and cautious response to their questions to mean that he at last was admitting, for the President, that Mr. Nixon wanted his Vice President's resignation and had so indicated at the September 25th meeting. A reporter's question to the Vice President, couched in these terms, caused him to say: "The President and I have not discussed that possibility. I want to make it very clear that I am not resigning." In a statement urging "all Americans to accord the Vice President the basic, decent consideration and presumption of innocence that are both his right and his due," the President conspicuously omitted any repetition of his previous and cruelly limited assertions of confidence that Mr. Agnew had done nothing wrong since he became Vice President. He also continued to avoid any reference to a request for or discussion of resignation.

Certain references in the attorney general's statement on the 25th and a point made by the Vice President's spokesman concerning resignation amount in my view to confirmation of news reports that resignation was discussed and strongly suggest that it came close to occurring. In acknowledging the truth of reports that he, Petersen and Prosecutor Beall met several times between September 12 and the 25th with three attorneys for the Vice President, Attorney General Richardson said the purpose of these meetings was to seek "prompt resolution of problems which might otherwise result in a constitutional dilemma of potentially serious consequences to the nation." Richardson then said, "It has proved impossible, *to this point* [my emphasis], to reconcile the Vice President's interests, as represented by his counsel, with the Department of Justice's perception of its responsibility to see that justice is pursued fully and fairly." In short the federal prosecutors and the Vice President's attorneys had been unable to strike the sort of plea-bargaining deal that was being rumored in news accounts.

Before and after the Richardson statement appeared there were speculative but seemingly substantive reports that the Vice President's lawyers discussed with the attorney general and his subordinates the possibility that Mr. Agnew might resign if he were either—depending on which account you read—assured that he wouldn't be prosecuted or let off with a plea of guilty to a minor charge. An Agnew spokesman denied that the Vice President had offered through his attorneys to resign on any terms. But the spokesman didn't deny that the possibility of resignation in return for some federal concession was discussed. He simply said that the Vice President and his attorneys had not initiated the discussion. This brings us back to Attorney General Richardson's reference to "a constitutional dilemma of potentially serious consequences to the nation." The dilemma in prospect would be brought about if the Vice President contended, as he had already indicated he might and as he promptly did in his letter to the speaker of the House, that "the Constitution bars a criminal proceeding of any kind—federal or state, county or town—against a President or Vice President while he holds office." Apart from the embarrassment resulting from criminal investigation and possible indictment of the Vice President, the President's attorneys had already staked out precisely that claim of constitutional immunity from criminal prosecution for Mr. Nixon, in connection with the Watergate scandals, and the last thing he could have wanted was a test of the proposition based on the weaker claim that a Vice President shares the immunity. It's conceivable, therefore, that the federal negotiators raised the possibility of a deal involving the Vice President's resignation and did so with the knowledge, implied if not explicit, that Mr. Nixon would be pleased if a deal could be worked out. The Attorney General took care to note in his statement that the negotiations with the Agnew attorneys had been undertaken "with the approval of the President's counsel and the President."

The Vice President's request for a House investigation of "charges" that could "assume the character of impeachable offenses" was a form of flight from the imminent prospect of federal grand jury investigation and indictment. His attorneys had indicated that they were thinking of asking a federal judge to prohibit the submission of evidence involving the Vice President to a federal grand jury in Maryland. A congressional investigation, had it been undertaken, would have strengthened the Agnew claim that he couldn't be indicted and prosecuted, or even investigated, until and unless he was impeached by the House, convicted by the Senate, and removed from office. Mr. Agnew delivered his letter in person to Speaker Albert, spent more than an hour at the capitol arguing his case with the speaker and other leaders of the Democratic majority, and must have realized afterward that there was very little chance that the Democrats would take him and President Nixon off the juridical hook. After further consultation the next day with leading Democratic congressmen, Speaker Albert effectively buried the Vice President's request that the House interpose itself between him and the federal prosecutors by saying nothing would be done so long as the matter was "before the courts." Agnew in his letter quoted the eighteenth-century concept that the House of Representatives in its impeachment role acts as "the grand inquest of the nation." Inquest in its modern meaning seemed more relevant to the Vice President's situation.

October 6, 1973

XXIX

Working It Out

In late September and early October, when the President and his principal associates appeared to have persuaded themselves that he was going to survive the scandals that continued to beset him and Vice President Agnew was saying that he would never resign and that the charges against him were "damned lies," the atmosphere at the Nixon White House was a strange mix of confidence and of a quality that was close to but not quite despair. The confidence arose in part from signs that the Senate Watergate committee's investigation was petering out and that the country in any event was bored with Watergate and all that it connoted; in part from a realization that a President, no matter how beleaguered, who was as determined as Mr. Nixon clearly was to hold onto his office and to make a show of power and impregnability had enormous advantages that were likely to be proof against worse troubles than any that this President had yet experienced or been threatened with. Sadness, frustration, helplessness were among the words that I heard used at the White House to describe a countervailing sense that recovery from the depths to which the President and his staff establishment were reduced last April and May could never be complete. It was a sense, a fear, that the prolonged process of rumor, suspicion, allegation and evidence of wrongdoing would never end. It seemed to the assistants whose accounts and impressions are reflected here, and it must have seemed to the President, that there was always something new in print or on the air that had to be denied, ignored or minimized.

The something new when Spiro Agnew succumbed and quit was a report, derived originally from testimony in civil suits against and involving Howard Hughes, the billionaire recluse, that the President's wealthy friend and occasional benefactor, C. G. (Bebe) Rebozo, accepted $100,000 in two cash payments from hirelings of Hughes in 1969 and 1970. Although the money was supposed to have been contributed for political campaign purposes, the report had it that Rebozo kept the $100,000 in cash in safety deposit boxes until he decided to return it to Hughes this year. Investigators for the Senate Watergate committee, the Internal Revenue Service and special Watergate prosecutor Archibald Cox looked into the matter. Deputy Press Secretary Gerald Warren was constrained to say for Mr. Nixon at the White House that "the President personally did not receive any such money." Warren declined to answer when he was asked whether the President was sufficiently interested in the report to ask his friend Bebe about it and about sworn testimony in the civil suits that Hughes regarded the payments as contributions to Mr. Nixon for his political benefit. It was at the President's personal insistence and orders that White House accounts of the purchase of his California estate at San Clemente omitted for more than three years any reference to the important parts that Rebozo and a much wealthier Nixon friend, Robert Abplanalp, played in financing an acquisition that the President, according to his own account, could not have managed without their help. The Rebozo-Hughes transaction was particularly embarrassing because the disclosure of it coincided with official reference to a characteristic that Richard Nixon and Spiro Agnew have in common. In a brutally detailed summary of the evidence of bribery, extortion and income tax evasion that federal prosecutors in Maryland were ready to bring against Agnew, the Department of Justice said that some of the

government witnesses attributed his readiness to accept cash payoffs when he was a county executive and governor of Maryland
to his belief "that his public position required him to adopt a
standard of living beyond his means."

There was understandable reluctance at the White House to
acknowledge the President's debt to the Senate Watergate committee and its staff. It was pleasanter and more heartening to put
the apparent waning of the Watergate investigation down to weakness of the case against the President and his administration than
it was to blame the committee's ineptitude. But one of the occasions for the revival of confidence around the President was in fact
a demonstration of that ineptitude. The President personally con-
gratulated and thanked Patrick Buchanan, a special consultant
and one of the few true believers and (conservative) ideologues
left on the Nixon staff of pragmatic doers and bumblers, upon his
televised performance before the committee. Buchanan routed his
interrogators with a hitherto unmatched display of bravado and
cynicism. He also provided an opportunity, which the committee
and its staff characteristically overlooked, to examine and challenge Mr. Nixon's basic assertion last April 30 that he could be
as ignorant as he claimed to be of the outrages that were perpetrated in his behalf during his 1972 campaign for reelection
because he had "to the maximum extent possible . . . sought to
delegate campaign operations, to remove the day-to-day campaign
decisions from the President's office and from the White House."
When Buchanan was asked why campaign memoranda that he had
written had been withheld from the committee on the ground that
they were privileged presidential documents, he answered: ". . .
I think that's not unreasonable in light of the fact that many of
the memoranda are to the President of the United States. Many
of the memoranda deal with recommendations for presidential
action. Many of the memoranda were prepared at the direction of
the President." Buchanan said later that his memos generally dealt
with overall campaign strategy and didn't contradict the President's
claim of detachment from campaign tactics. I continue to believe,
however, though I cannot prove, that the persisting strain of
unease and uncertainty at the White House arises in some part
from unacknowledged awareness that the President's protective

version of his campaign role is false and subject to exposure and disproof that would be disastrous for him.

It was in this atmosphere of mingled confidence and apprehension around the President that Spiro Agnew approached, fought off, backed away from and finally accepted a deal with his prospective prosecutors and, certainly in an ultimate and probably in a literal sense, with his President. At a press conference in Washington the day after Agnew resigned and, without pleading guilty, admitted his guilt in one instance of income tax evasion, Attorney General Elliot Richardson removed any cause for doubt that the President concluded last summer, after he learned that serious charges against his Vice President were in the making, that his—Mr. Nixon's—best interests would be served if he got rid of his Vice President. Richardson did this when he said that Fred Buzhardt, one of the President's White House lawyers, initiated the bargaining with Agnew's attorneys. He said that Buzhardt first asked the attorney general whether he was willing to work out a deal with the Vice President's lawyers and that, throughout the subsequent negotiations, Mr. Nixon approved "the general direction and the fundamental basis on which the matter was being handled." The President said on August 22 that he believed Agnew to be innocent of any wrongdoing after he became Vice President and on October 3 that "the charges . . . do not relate in any way to his activities as Vice President." This was true of the formal charges but not of the evidence that the Justice Department summarized and published on October 10. According to that evidence Vice President Agnew sought and accepted substantial cash sums from Maryland contractors after he was inaugurated in 1969. It was desperately important to the President, one gathers, that his Vice President be formally accused and convicted only of offenses that were committed before he became Richard Nixon's man.

Spiro Agnew, that valiant exponent of the work ethic and of Nixonian law and order, is in disgrace, gone from the administration, on probation for three years and liable to federal imprisonment during that period if he misbehaves. He has, as the attorney general said in justifying the negotiated deal, saved the Nixon presidency and the country from a rending time of prosecution and trial. The crushing record of extorted and welcomed bribes that the Justice Department summary of the evidence sets forth makes sorrow for Agnew impossible and the compassion that the attorney general recommends difficult. There will be cries—there were some at the attorney general's explanatory press conference—that the lenient treatment of Agnew demonstrates once again that the law is kinder to the powerful than it is to the weak. A fair judgment is that the country is well rid of a crooked Vice President and fortunate in being spared the agony of a criminal trial or impeachment proceeding. In the wake of Agnew's going a proper prayer is that the President who so dismally failed in 1968 and 1972 to offer the electorate a fit and qualified vice-presidential nominee come up now with a successor who is fit to be President and who deserves the necessary approval of the House and Senate. For the choice, after all, we are dependent upon a President who until quite recently was asking some of his assistants how they rated the chances that he might be impeached and removed from office.

October 20, 1973

Nightmares

There Agnew was on television, speaking with mawkish self-pity of his "nightmare-come-true" and at the end saying "thank you, good night and farewell" in a sepulchral tone that made some viewers wonder whether he was saying farewell to life. The remarkable thing was that it was so easy, so soon after Spiro T. Agnew resigned and asked a federal judge to find and declare him a felon in order to escape indictment and probable conviction for many more and larger felonies, to adjust without amazement, satisfaction or regret to the fact that this man was no longer the Vice President and potentially the next President of the United States. It was almost as if he had never been what he became in 1969 and remained until he was found out and brought down in 1973: the embodiment in the minds and hopes of millions of Americans of the rectitude, the order, the simple dedication to simple rightness that they missed in their society and were led by Agnew to believe they had been done out of by elitist snobs and grubby malcontents.

The President who had plucked Agnew from the sewer of

Maryland politics and conferred him upon the nation behaved and had his spokesmen talk as if he wanted his sometime Vice President to be forgotten and banished from the public mind as soon as possible. Agnew in his televised farewell spoke of "a great President." He thanked Mr. Nixon for "his attempt to be both fair to me and faithful to his oath of office" and for "the restraint and the compassion which he has demonstrated." He also let a friendly interviewer, Frank Van der Linden of the *Nashville Banner,* portray him as a broken and embittered victim who felt that he had been unfairly driven from office. The contradiction was more apparent than real. Agnew must have known since early August, when the first news of his involvement in a federal investigation of Maryland corruption was published, that the President wanted him out of office and out of the Nixon administration. But it's believably said at the White House that the President got him out without ordering him to quit or confronting him with an explicit ultimatum.

One of Mr. Nixon's staff counsellors, former Congressman and Defense Secretary Melvin Laird, admits now that he began warning congressional Republicans in early August that the evidence against Agnew was serious and substantial. Counsellor Bryce Harlow, one of Agnew's few friends in the Nixon inner circle, and J. Fred Buzhardt, a White House lawyer, were assigned by the President in mid-September to convince Senator Barry Goldwater that any public defense of Agnew would be futile and foolish. They were ordered to summarize for Goldwater the accumulated evidence that Agnew had solicited and taken money from Maryland contractors before and after he became Vice President. Senator Hugh Scott, the Republican floor leader, indicated to other Republican senators on the implied authority of the President that they could soon be sitting in judgment of an impeached Vice President and that they therefore had better be cautious in discussing the matter. While Agnew was being deprived of congressional support in this fashion, not necessarily in a vindictive effort to destroy him but certainly to minimize foreseen embarrassment to the administration and the Republican Party, Fred Buzhardt was arranging and managing negotiations between Agnew's lawyers and Justice Department prosecutors for a bargained plea. This maneuver almost succeeded in September and finally did in October, when Agnew realized that the evidence against him and the web woven around him were more than he could overcome or escape. His cry in a speech on September 29 that "if indicted I will not resign" was not the promise of indefinite defiance that it was understood to be at the time. Agnew had known for weeks that the President wanted his resignation. His assertion on the 29th was his way of saying to Mr. Nixon and to Attorney General Elliot Richardson, who said later that the President approved every major step in the plea negotiations, that the President could have the desired resignation only if the Vice President were let off without indictment, trial and predictable imprisonment. That's the way it ended—with a $10,000 fine, probation for three years, and a pledge of no further federal prosecution in return for the resignation and Agnew's assent to the publication of utterly damning evidence that he'd been taking money from Maryland contractors for 10 years and was still doing it in December of 1972.

The President's choice of a successor to Agnew is of such numbing ordinariness that I've nothing to say about its merits except that it should have been better and could have been worse. Congressman Gerald Ford of Michigan has been reciting the virtues of Richard Nixon and of his legislative proposals once a week in the White House press room since 1969 and I've yet to hear him say anything that was memorably bright, critical of the President, or indicative of profound understanding of anything. I was impressed in 1969 with Representative Ford's cool and intelligent estimate, provided in a private interview, of the abilities and attitudes then prevailing at the Nixon White House, and repelled by his savage and shoddy attempt to bring about the impeachment of Associate Justice William O. Douglas. What I find interesting at the moment is the way in which the President went about or anyhow professed to go about the choice.

A key fact to be kept in mind is that Mr. Nixon must have anticipated since late July or early August that he'd have to nominate a successor Vice President who could be confirmed by majority vote in the House and Senate without a damaging fight. Was the President's elaborate show of canvassing many possibilities, and reducing them to five and two and finally to Ford, for real or was it a charade? "All I can tell you," one of the senior participants in the exercise said while it was going on, "is that he's acting as if it's for real." Melvin Laird said after the choice was announced that he asked Ford several weeks ago whether he'd want the nomination. This indicates but hardly proves that it was a charade. One of the few established facts is that the President didn't ask Laird, Bryce Harlow or his third counsellor, Anne Armstrong of Texas, to tell him whom they preferred and tell him why they did. So far as is known Mr. Nixon didn't invite or tolerate in-person or face-to-face discussion and argument with anybody, on his staff or in Congress or among the party leaders. He instructed his staff chief, General Alexander Haig, to instruct other senior assistants, including the three counsellors, to put down three choices, in order of preference, and to submit the lists to him through Haig—*unsigned.* It seems to be true, though one of the President's wisest and closest advisers finds it hard to believe, that he never personally discussed the choice with John B. Connally, who completed his turn from Democrat to Nixocrat to Republican early this year and has Mr. Nixon's promise of support for the Republican presidential nomination in 1976. Haig discussed the Agnew succession with Connally twice, by telephone, with the end result that Mr. Nixon and Connally communicated their agreement with each other to each other through Haig that it would be better to save Big John for 1976 and duck the bruising struggle in Congress that would have resulted if he'd been proposed for Vice President. Connally indicated to at least one unofficial friend in Washington that he hoped the President would pick Governor Nelson Rockefeller, who is likely to be a principal contender for the presidential nomination in 1976. Connally calculated that three years as Mr. Nixon's second Vice President would probably finish off Rockefeller or anybody else as a serious 1976 contender. Rockefeller was foolish enough to want the vice presidency and he figured in one of the four announcement drafts that the President had his speech writers prepare.

Mr. Nixon indicated to Ford but didn't quite tell him on the morning of October 12 that he was the choice. Ford was also told that he might be getting a telephone call from Haig. At about

7:30 P.M. the President telephoned Ford and told him that Haig had something to tell him, which Haig did after calling back on another line with an extension so that Mrs. Ford could share the moment with her husband. She was told to stay out of sight at the White House and out of the White House East Room, where the choice was announced at 9 P.M., until it was announced, so that her presence wouldn't tip off the assembled dignitaries and the media. The President had his surprise and his fun, with a televised display of pomp and power that seemed to me to be singularly vulgar and inappropriate. Spiro Agnew and the occasion for the nomination of Gerald Ford were not mentioned.

October 27, 1973

XXXI

To the Brink

Here is the gist of the story, to the extent that it was known on October 24, of the President's steady, deliberate, calculated march to the brink of ruin during the nine days that began on October 15. What is meant by deliberate calculation is that every step along the ruinous way was carefully considered by the President and by assistants and consultants who are reputed to be among the brainiest men in his service. Only one of the consequences, the discharge of special Watergate prosecutor Archibald Cox and the transfer of his staff and functions to the Department of Justice, was foreseen and intended. Among the consequences that were not foreseen and not intended, and that therefore reflect in the most serious fashion upon the President's judgment and upon his capacity to govern the country, were the resignations of Attorney General Elliot Richardson and Deputy Attorney General William Ruckelshaus; the instant and enormous increase in public and congressional demand for the resignation or impeachment of the President; and, in a desperate reversal and maneuver to save himself and his presidency, his abject surrender to the orders of two courts that he turn over to a federal judge the taped recordings of presidential conversations that could either convict or acquit him of complicity in and concealment of Watergate crimes ranging from burglary, political espionage and subornation of perjury to the illegal collection and felonious misuse of campaign funds.

The calculations and decisions that led to these consequences sprang from an aspect of the White House atmosphere that I described in *The New Republic*'s October 20 issue: a sense and a fear that the President and his staff establishment could never recover completely from the demoralizing effects of the Watergate scandals and that the prolonged process of rumor, suspicion, allegation and evidence of wrongdoing would never end. I assumed but didn't know in early October that Mr. Nixon shared this sense of frustration and apprehension with the assistants who expressed it. The accounts and explanations, publicly and privately given, of the events that the President set in train on the 15th indicated that he not only shared it but suffered from it to a greater degree than most and perhaps all of his senior associates did. It appears from the accounts and explanations relied upon here that Mr. Nixon decided during the weekend preceding Monday, October 15, that he had to end what he called "this hemorrhage," referring to the remorseless drainage of his credibility and prestige, and that in order to end it he had to do two things. One of them was to back away from and compromise his previously adamant insistence that neither Congress nor the courts had the right and power to compel him or any President to disclose taped or written records of presidential conversations and transactions. He also decided that he had to abolish or at the very least neutralize the independent Watergate special prosecution force that the Senate Judiciary Committee compelled him to let his third attorney general, Elliot Richardson, set up outside the Department of Justice and under Archibald Cox last May. Both of these objectives were pursued secretly, simultaneously and by the same means until the first of them was acknowledged and briefly boasted about. The second objective was never acknowledged. It was not convincingly denied, either, and it was made known by covert leakage from the White House staff for a reason that says a good deal, all of it depressing, about the plight and nature of the Nixon presidency.

The reason was that Nixon assistants deemed it necessary to prove to the media and to the public that the President was neither off his rocker nor afraid that he would be shown to have been a party to illegal and impeachable behavior if Cox and his staff of prosecutors were allowed to continue their investigations with the zeal and vigor they were displaying and to seek and obtain evidence from White House files in support of their allegations.

Public and congressional reaction to the firing of Cox and the resignations of Richardson and Ruckelshaus indicated to Nixon assistants that the President was widely thought to have acted rashly and foolishly, in a fit of pique at best and of irrational frustration and anger at worst. Nothing vexes the President's associates and, one may suspect, Mr. Nixon himself, more than the impression dating from his early years in politics that behind a mask of phenomenally rigid self-control he is unduly excitable, emotionally insecure and unstable, and likely to crack under extreme pressure unless he watches himself and conserves his energies very carefully. Some of Mr. Nixon's past characterizations of himself and occasional instances of his observed behavior tend to validate the impression. In any case the sense of vulnerability that the impression causes contributed to a conclusion at the White House that the evidently widespread notion that the President had acted impulsively and out of fear had to be rebutted immediately and strongly. The rebuttal was conveyed to reporters by the sort of unattributable leaks that the President's people resent and deplore when he is the victim. It was to the effect that the decision to remove or vitiate the special prosecutor and his crew of zealots was taken with the greatest deliberation, for absolutely necessary reasons, and was implemented coolly and skillfully. Far from arising from irrational anger, the story went, the effort and outcome were examples of Nixon planning and execution at their best.

The fundamental reason offered was that the Nixon presidency could not survive if it continued to be subjected to reports of new allegations and investigations and to constant demands for evidence from the President's confidential files. According to the White House story, the apprehended danger to the President and his presidency was not that the allegations were certain or likely to be proven true. It was rather the dreadful erosion of confidence —public confidence in the President and his administration, and the confidence of the President and his officials in themselves— that was so clearly occurring and increasing. It could not be factually alleged, and was not alleged, that the special prosecutor and his staff originated most of these reports. By comparison with the staff of the Senate Watergate investigating committee, for instance, the Cox staff had been a model of discretion. But, in the White House view, the mere existence of the special prosecution force and the announced scope of its investigations contributed to a general impression that the Watergate evils already exposed were as nothing by comparison with the evils yet to be exposed and proven. It was the special prosecutor's suit for access to nine of the Nixon tapes that was forcing that explosive issue and the President's claim of executive privilege and protected confidentiality toward decision in the Supreme Court. As Mr. Nixon and his associates saw things, it was the special prosecutor who was putting the President in the wretched position of appearing to maintain while having to deny that he was above the law and capable of defying court orders. Beyond all else the knowledge at the White House that the special prosecutor and his staff were seeking indictments and preparing for trials that would involve Nixon friends and associates, past and present, in numbers and on a scale that would keep the Watergate scandal and its extensions in the public mind throughout the President's second term compounded his decision that the Cox operation had to be terminated.

Here we encounter a kind of madness, a contradiction that the purveyors of the White House explanation did not even try to reconcile. The contradiction lay in the claim that the President's purpose was not actually to halt or limit proper investigations and prosecutions, but only to bring the process of investigation and prosecution back where Mr. Nixon and his lawyers thought it belonged, within the Department of Justice and under his and his attorney general's control. In order to accomplish this purpose the President had Attorney General Richardson go through the motions of trying to negotiate an agreement with Archibald Cox that neither Mr. Nixon nor Elliot Richardson could possibly have

expected Cox to accept and work under. There are two versions of this projected and aborted agreement, Elliot Richardson's and Richard Nixon's. Richardson proposed to Cox that he settle for submission to a federal court and to a Watergate grand jury of summaries of nine Nixon tapes instead of insisting on compliance with orders of Judge John Sirica and of a federal appellate court that Judge Sirica be allowed to examine the original tapes and excerpt pertinent Watergate material from them. The President indicated in his version that Richardson also proposed to Cox that he submit to and obey an order that he seek no other tapes or records of presidential conversations and actions. Richardson made no such proposal. Instead he insisted throughout five days of negotiation with Cox and with the White House assistants and lawyers who were acting for the President that the question of further requests for presidential tapes and documents be postponed. The attorney general's effort to avert a conclusive confrontation between Cox and the President seems to have led to some ambiguity and to an impression among the President's people that Richardson would go along with, even if he would not explicitly convey, an order to Cox to halt his demands for presidential evidence. However that may have been, the President and his agents certainly knew throughout the proceeding that Archibald Cox, a famously independent and touchy character, would never submit to such an order.

On the sixth day, in the first of the only two personal meetings and talks that Richardson had with the President throughout the whole affair, the attorney general told Mr. Nixon directly what he'd been telling General Alexander Haig, the staff chief, and the President's lawyers. This was that Cox would not accept a flat order to limit his investigations and demands for White House evidence, that Richardson would convey no such order to Cox and that he, Richardson, would resign rather than dismiss Cox. I say "told"; Richardson may have, as he intimated at a press conference, relied in part upon admonitions and warnings that he had previously conveyed to the President through Haig and the lawyers. The point is that Mr. Nixon could not have been under any misapprehension when he ordered General Haig to order Richardson to fire Cox and Richardson resigned, and when he then had General Haig order Deputy Attorney General Ruckelshaus to fire Cox and Ruckelshaus resigned. Solicitor General Robert Bork, the acting attorney general by statutory succession, fired Cox. Shaken and shocked by the stormy reaction, Mr. Nixon soon announced his complete compliance with the appellate court's order to give Judge Sirica the nine tapes Cox had tried to subpoena, and an impression spread that the resignations and the firing would have been averted if the President had only announced full compliance in the first place. This impression was in error. Elliot Richardson stated the essence of the matter at his press conference when he said: "The President was very deliberate, very restrained in my meeting with him, but he was absolutely firm on the course he had determined upon."

It was said at the start of this report that only the dismissal of Archibald Cox was intended and that the resignations of Richardson and Ruckelshaus, with the consequent shocks to the country and to any confidence in Richard Nixon that may have remained by then, were not intended. Madness would have had to prevail at the White House if the resignations were either intended from the first or invited at the last. They were invited.

November 3, 1973

————

This account understated the personal antipathy at the White House to Prosecutor Cox and his zealous assistants and, at the end, the President's cold and miscalculated willingness to let Richardson and Ruckelshaus go with Cox.

XXXII

Risk and Retribution

There's a certain relief and pleasure in turning for once from the unceasing run of presidential horrors to a couple of current books about the presidency as an institution. Both Emmet John Hughes in *The Living Presidency* (Coward, McCann & Geoghegan; $10.50) and Arthur M. Schlesinger, Jr., in *The Imperial Presidency* (Houghton Mifflin; $10) deal with the incumbent President as well as with the institution, and neither of them is kind to Richard Nixon. But both of them remind us of a fact that is too often and easily overlooked in this time of deepening trouble for the President and for the country, when senators are calling upon Mr. Nixon to resign and a committee of the House of Representatives is considering whether he should be impeached. The fact is that the sins and excesses of the Nixon presidency, or anyhow the opportunity and the power to commit the sins and excesses, have their roots in a past that goes back to the nation's eighteenth century founders and to the period that Emmet Hughes calls "that season gray with doubt, when the Republic was being born."

The origins, growth and what both authors hold to have been

in the Nixon time an outrageous distortion and misuse of presidential power are the central subjects and preoccupations of these books. A refreshing distinction of the Hughes book is that it contains no reference to Watergate and the scandals related to it. For Hughes, the prime contemporary manifestation of presidential power improperly perceived, inflated and applied is the Vietnam war. His concern and strictures have to do with "the pattern of presidential action and leadership throughout the Vietnam war" and not merely with the Nixon phase. He ascribes to Lyndon Johnson no less than to Richard Nixon the deceit of the public and Congress, the misjudgments of Asian communism, the habit of blaming the critics rather than the promoters and proponents of the war for the harm it did, and the other products of executive arrogance that marked its course. Hughes discerns in the secrecy, silence and solitude that cloaked the President's actions and decisions during the last months of American participation in the Vietnam portion of the Indochina war an example of the danger that Edward S. Corwin wrote about in 1941 when he observed that "no President has a mandate from the Constitution to conduct our foreign relations according to his own sweet will." Yet, for all the abuses of presidential power that Hughes recounts and deplores, he winds up in agreement with Henry Stimson's finding that Presidents Theodore and Franklin Roosevelt were effective leaders because they understood and enjoyed the use of power and with the dictum of Demosthenes that "as a general marches at the head of his troops, so ought wise politicians . . . to march at the head of affairs."

Arthur Schlesinger acknowledges at the start of this, his tenth book of political history and analysis, that circumstances have compelled or seemed to compel much of the concentration of power in the presidency that he traces from Washington to Nixon and that "historians and political scientists, this writer among them, contributed to the rise of the presidential mystique." Like Hughes, he has to grant that effective Presidents are strong Presidents and, also like Hughes, he is at his weakest when he tries to define curbs upon the expansion and use of presidential power. Schlesinger, in fact, falls back for this purpose mostly upon a summary of some rather tattered remedies that Senator Sam Ervin

has proposed. Even so, Schlesinger is interesting and worth reading when he examines the origins and evolution of what he variously calls "the imperial presidency" and, in its extreme perver-
sions under Richard Nixon, "the runaway presidency," "the
plebiscitary presidency" and "the revolutionary presidency."

This reader gathers that Schlesinger set out originally to write
a "history of the war-making power," documenting his thesis that
"the imperial presidency received its decisive impetus . . . from
the capture by the presidency of the most vital of national decisions, the decision to go to war," and in mid-composition let himself be trapped by time and events into dealing also with the
complex of evils known as Watergate. The effect is to give an
excellent book the appearance of instant history, below the author's
usual standard of quality. But the effect is fortunate, too, in that
we have in this book a thoughtful analysis of Watergate as a
wretched but understandable phenomenon.

The various characterizations of the Nixon presidency already
quoted—"runaway" and "plebiscitary," the last meaning that Mr.
Nixon truly did interpret his 1972 victory to be a mandate to do
whatever he pleased—bring Schlesinger to his "revolutionary presidency" and to his conclusion that "Richard M. Nixon, for all
his conventionality of utterance and mind, really was a genuine
revolutionary." Interestingly and quite possibly with great pre-
science, Schlesinger in this and other passages refers to Mr. Nixon
and his presidency in the past tense. The "new American revolution" proclaimed by the President in 1971 and dismissed by this
reporter, among others, as an empty and foredoomed exercise,
was in the view presented here a genuine attempt at revolution by
a serious revolutionary, Richard Nixon. "But the essence of this
revolution was not, as he said at the time, power to the people.
The essence was power to the presidency." Schlesinger sees in it a
revolution "aimed at reducing the power of Congress at every point
along the line and moving toward rule by presidential decree." It
may, in the most charitable interpretation, have arisen from "a
considered judgment that the old separation of powers had out-
lived its time" and had "so frustrated government on behalf of
the majority that the constitutional system had become finally in-
tolerable." However that may have been, it meant that Richard

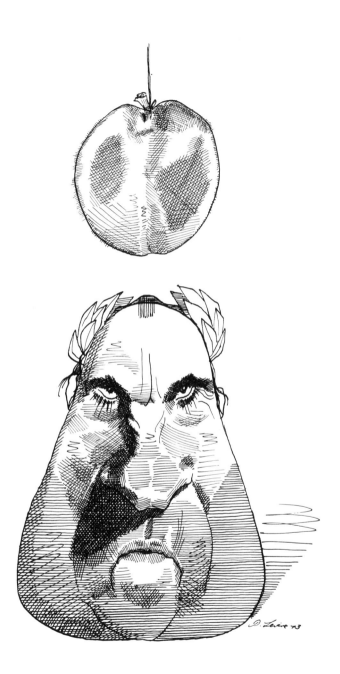

Nixon had come to embody and propagate a theory—expressed
specifically in his 1970 internal security plan—that "the President
of the United States, on his own personal and secret finding of
emergency, had the right to nullify the Constitution and the law."
Schlesinger quotes Justice Brandeis' remark that governments
which commit crimes in order to convict criminals invite "terrible
retribution" and then writes: "Retribution came, and its name
was Watergate. But it came almost by accident. Watergate was
a probable, but by no means a necessary, consequence of the effort to change the nature of the presidency." Guessing that Mr.
Nixon "might have carried his revolution . . . very far indeed"
if he'd avoided the kind of excesses of illegal activity that he
authorized in 1970, Schlesinger explains the mistake in personal
terms: ". . . his revolution took direction and color not just from
the external circumstances pressing new powers on the presidency
but from the drives and needs of his own agitated psyche. This
was the fatal flaw in the revolutionary design. For everywhere he
looked he saw around him hideous threats to the national security.
. . . If his public actions led toward a scheme of presidential
supremacy under a considerably debilitated Constitution, his private obsessions pushed him toward the view that the presidency
could set itself, at will, *above* the Constitution. It was this theory
that led straight to Watergate."

When Schlesinger closed out his book in the early autumn of
1973, it seemed to him that Mr. Nixon "still failed to understand
that the sickness of his presidency had been caused, not by the
overzealousness of his friends nor by the malice of his enemies,
but by the expansion and abuse of presidential power in itself."
Arthur Schlesinger could not, as a conscientious historian, ascribe
it all solely to Richard Nixon's personal defects. He wrote:
"Nixon's presidency was not an aberration but a culmination. It
carried to reckless extremes a compulsion toward presidential
power rising out of deep-running changes in the foundations of
society. In a time of the acceleration of history and the decay of
traditional institutions and values, a strong presidency was both
a greater necessity than ever before and a greater risk—necessary
to hold a spinning and distracted society together, necessary to

make the separation of powers work, risky because of the awful temptation held out to override the separation of powers and burst the bonds of the Constitution. The nation required both a strong presidency for leadership and the separation of powers for liberty."

What to do about a President who exploits these contradictory requirements as Richard Nixon has? The answer suggested in this book is—impeach.

November 10, 1973

XXXIII

Not Yet, Not Now

Between October 26, when the President said at his 35th press conference that "I am going to continue to do this job," and November 5 and 6, when two of Mr. Nixon's spokesmen said for him that "the President is not a quitter" and that "the President has absolutely no intention of leaving this job until it's finished," there was a torrent of comment by journalists and noticeably less comment by politicians to the effect that he ought to resign for his own and the country's good. *Time,* columnist Joseph Alsop, *The New York Times, The Detroit News, The Denver Post* and Republican Edward Brooke of Massachusetts, the only black member of the United States Senate, said that Mr. Nixon should quit. Republican Senators Barry Goldwater of Arizona, Peter Dominick of Colorado and Hugh Scott of Pennsylvania, the party's Senate floor leader, and Senator James Buckley of New York, an independent conservative, said or indicated in varying ways that the President had lost the confidence of the country and was losing his capacity to govern. Remarks of this sort, headlined and broadcast along with outright calls for resignation and polls showing a steady fall in public trust, stimulated the spread of expectations close to certainty that the Nixon presidency was going to end, sooner or later and probably sooner, with impeachment if it didn't end with resignation. A reader who is an inmate of the federal penitentiary in Atlanta assumed in a letter to me that the annual collection of these pieces to be published in book form next year would have to be entitled *The Last Nixon Watch*. I'd thought that I was pretty smart when I suggested as much to the publisher's editors in New York, only to find that they were already planning along that line and thought that *they* were mighty smart.

The spate of calls for resignation had a backlash effect upon me and, it turned out, upon other journalists who are no more predisposed in Richard Nixon's favor than I am. My gut reaction was that there was something premature, wrong and unjust about this sudden burst of conviction and assumption that the President was totally and irremediably guilty as charged. That's what the calls for resignation really said, it seemed to me, although they were generally couched in less direct and inculpatory terms. They suggested that if most people thought the President was guilty and had withdrawn their trust and confidence from him, he might as well be guilty whether he was or not and therefore ought to get out.

As one who has been writing since 1968 that Mr. Nixon is a fundamentally shoddy type, not worthy of the presidency and worthy of praise only when he rises above his past and himself to uncharacteristic levels of purpose and attainment, and since the autumn of 1972 that he surely knew more about and did more than he has said he did to conceal the antisocial thuggeries that we have in mind when we say "Watergate," I may be considered and indeed am considered at the White House to be a minor fomenter of and contributor to the corrosive and deepening condition of disbelief in Richard Nixon. Nevertheless, and however open to a charge of hypocrisy and journalistic license the assertion may lay me, I hold that neither the case for resignation nor the case for impeachment has been made.

It is terribly easy for the journalist to fall into sloppy terminology in discussing these matters. For example I wrote in this journal's last issue that the House Judiciary Committee is considering whether the President should be impeached. In fact, and there is a substantial difference, the committee is considering whether the House should consider whether he should be impeached. It is one thing for a reporter and commentator such as myself to say, as I did last May in connection with Mr. Nixon's first major Watergate explanation and apologia on April 30, that he elided, evaded and lied when he said he stayed so far away from the management of his 1972 reelection campaign that he couldn't have known and hence didn't know of the wrongs perpetrated for him during the campaign. I deduced from what I believed then and still believe to be adequate indicators that this was so. But it's another thing to act upon or demand that others act upon a deduction of this kind when such investigative bodies as the Senate's special Watergate committee have been too inept, too lazy, or too afraid of the truth to make the inquiries necessary to demonstrate whether—I'd say *that*—it is so.

The latest trigger for the conviction and assertions that the President should resign is the horrifying disclosure that two of the nine White House recordings subpoenaed by the fired special Watergate prosecutor, Archibald Cox, and required by two courts to be submitted to federal Judge John Sirica, are missing from the President's storage bin. They could prove or disprove former Attorney General John Mitchell's assertion that the President indicated no prior knowledge whatever of the original Watergate burglary and bugging when Mitchell first discussed it with him by telephone on June 20 of last year, and former White House Counsel John Wesley Dean's sworn testimony that in a talk with him last April 15 Mr. Nixon showed that he had known for months about the Watergate cover-up and about, among other things, bribes intended to purchase the silence of some of the Watergate defendants. The White House story is that because of flukes— a tape ran out; the President talked with Mitchell on an unrecorded White House telephone line—the recordings never existed. The President, among a very few others at the White House, has known since September 29 and may have known since last June that the two tapes were missing. Yet his lawyers had been telling judges and his spokesmen had been telling the media for weeks that all nine of the demanded tapes were intact and secure. Mr. Nixon staked his repute as late as October 19 on a qualified offer to make summaries of all of them available to Judge Sirica and the Senate Watergate committee. Instead of preparing the media, the public and the courts in advance for the fact that two of the most critical tapes were missing, the President and his people let the news break like thunder upon the public when Judge Sirica disclosed it on October 31.

On its face the White House story is incredible. It is widely and deservedly disbelieved. The flaws in it further and support an impression that the missing tapes were destroyed because they incriminated Mr. Nixon. Yet, despite four years and more of instruction in the perils of giving Mr. Nixon and his official apologists the benefit of doubt in critical matters, I at this writing believe the White House story and do not include it and the circumstance that it purports to explain among the arguable reasons for demanding resignation or impeachment. My primary reason for believing it is that Leonard Garment, the White House counsel who succeeded John Dean, is among the Nixon lawyers vouching for the story to Judge Sirica. My judgment of Garment is that he wouldn't be doing that and wouldn't still be at the White House if he had not satisfied himself that the story is true. A secondary reason for believing the story is that, for it to be true, a whole troop of characters beginning with the President and including his staff chief, General Alexander Haig, have to have been guilty of stupidity on a colossal scale. One of the few safe and proven rules for a reporter working at the Nixon White House is: never underestimate the Nixon establishment's capacity for stupidity, especially in its upper levels.

Other journalists who were driven to second thought by the rash of calls for resignation and were mentioned earlier in this report include the editors of *The Washington Post* and Tom Wicker, a *New York Times* columnist, who is referred to at the White House as "that bastard Wicker." It's fair to say, I think, that neither the *Post* in its news and editorial columns nor Wicker in his signed column pause very often to note that the Watergate case against Mr. Nixon is considerably less than complete. In their discussions of resignation, they did pause for that purpose. Thus Wicker:

"Resignation would in no way resolve the question of Nixon's guilt or innocence; it would not even leave a clear sense of what the charges were, or should have been; and while resignation would remove him from office, it would not necessarily terminate his case." And the *Post:* ". . . those who cry 'resign' are asking Mr. Nixon to leave office without a formal, final resolution one way or another of allegations that have been, or might be, made against him." Wicker's and the *Post* editors' main points are that trial in the Senate after impeachment by the House is the sole means provided by the constitution for the determination of an incumbent President's guilt or innocence and that Mr. Nixon could, if forced from office without such a determination, keep a belief that he was done in by leftist and media conspirators alive for years. Those who advocate impeachment rather than resignation for these kinds of reasons are somewhat in the position of aboriginal Indians who, in historic fable, could have solved the problems raised by a troublesome captive by letting him escape but preferred to hold him until they were ready to burn him at the stake. Anyhow, those who recoil from immediate resignation and say as I do—not yet, not now—have a point.

November 17, 1973

———

George D. Aiken of Vermont, the reticent and respected dean of Senate Republicans, said in a rare floor speech the day after the foregoing went to press that "the developing hue and cry for the President's resignation suggests to me a veritable epidemic of emotionalism"; observed that "the White House has handled its domestic troubles with . . . relentless incompetence"; and concluded: "May I now pass on to this Congress advice which I received from a fellow Vermonter—'Either impeach him or get off his back.' "

XXXIV

Counterattack

On the afternoon of November 8, the day after Mr. Nixon acknowledged at the end of a televised speech about the energy crisis that "great numbers of Americans have had doubts raised about the integrity of the President of the United States" and declared that he had "no intention whatever" of resigning, one of his senior assistants said three times during a 40-minute conversation that he was sure that the President could solve his problems of confidence and authority "if he wanted to." The suggestion, twice repeated, that Mr. Nixon might not "want to" caused me to ask the assistant whether he was implying a doubt that the President really wanted and intended to stick it out. Oh no, the assistant said; all he meant was that he wasn't sure that the President was willing to do the particular things that the assistant thought he'd have to do in order to halt the erosion of trust. A similar experience on the same afternoon with another assistant who was assigned to think up suggestions for the President and didn't know how they were being received provided a further measure of the uneasiness and uncertainty that pervaded the

Nixon White House behind the President's announced determination to meet his appalling array of Watergate problems "head on."

A minor reason for the unease around the President was his isolation from most of his staff, including most of his senior staff. It continued to be true, as I've been reporting since last summer, that the only assistants with whom he regularly spent useful amounts of time were General Alexander Haig, the staff chief who replaced H. R. Haldeman last May, and Press Secretary Ronald Ziegler, who actually functioned as a press secretary and spokesman for a few days in early November but since last July has served the President mostly in private as a trusted and trusting friend and listener. It was said for Mr. Nixon, and truly enough, that he'd always been that way, preferring to deal directly with as few people as he possibly could and, before the Watergate storm hit him and his White House last April 30, relying upon Haldeman and the departed John Ehrlichman much as he relies now upon Haig and Ziegler. But the explanation didn't suffice. In a time of stress and doubt, extending from the inner White House to the nation at large, too many ranking assistants knew only secondhand, through Haig and Ziegler, or didn't know at all what their President was planning and thinking and how he was bearing up. His isolation from them made them more vulnerable than they otherwise would have been to a couple of far more serious causes of uneasiness and uncertainty.

One cause was a fear amounting to an assumption that the worst of the Watergate scandals were yet to break upon the President and them. The numbing succession of scandals and allegations of scandal that had already struck was enough in itself to account for the assumption that the crushing sequence couldn't have ended and was never going to end. But a related and, for the President and for the morale of the Nixon establishment, a more disastrous factor underlay the tensions and anxieties. The clear though unacknowledged fact was that confidence in the President's integrity and wisdom had all but vanished among his own assistants. Nothing else could explain the fact that the most emphatic assertions in private of belief that the President was going to survive the scandals, the demands for his resignation and the threats of impeachment invariably ended with some such remark as, "That is, of course, if something else doesn't break." Counsellor Melvin Laird, the former congressman and secretary of Defense who joined the White House staff in July and is saying that he's quitting as soon as Gerald Ford, the President's nominee for Vice President to succeed Spiro Agnew, is confirmed by majorities of the House and Senate, contributed to the apprehension of dire things to come with an argument that he is using on senators and representatives. He tells Republicans and Democrats alike that they've got to confirm Gerald Ford without delay because another Watergate crunch, maybe worse than any yet experienced, is coming soon. He is saying that a confirmed Vice President ought to be in place when it does, ready to help the President withstand it. Laird doesn't quite say in addition that a Republican Vice President has got to be in office, ready to replace Mr. Nixon when and if he resigns or is impeached and removed. But that's the impression he leaves.

At meetings with 192 House Republicans and later with some 30 of the most influential Republican congressmen, the key question thrown at Counsellor Bryce Harlow about the President's plight and prospects was "Can he govern?" Harlow recalls that he answered the question approximately as follows: "I can't answer that. The President can't answer it. Only you gentlemen can answer it. If you stay with him, stand by him, support him—*of course he can govern*. If you don't stay with him, if you desert him —of course he can't govern." At the time in early November, Harlow was hoping that the President would go on the counter-offensive, holding more and regular press conferences; answering a particular Watergate or Watergate-related charge at each press session and inviting questions on any and all other charges; show himself in Washington and around the country in the act of being an aggressive and confident President; and, beyond all else, have members of Congress, singly and in groups, at the White House to see him and go to them on Capitol Hill, talking and listening to them and showing them that he cared about them. Well into the first fortnight of November, Harlow hadn't discussed these ideas directly with the President. Neither had Patrick Buchanan, who was thinking along the same lines and firing memos to the President

through General Haig. The President took Harlow with him to
Florida on November 1, talked briefly with him on the presidential
plane en route from and back to Washington, and didn't see or
speak to him during four days at Key Biscayne. Harlow isn't saying
what they talked about on the plane, except that it wasn't his ideas
for defensive counterattack. Close to a week after the return, Harlow still hadn't had or made a chance to discuss his ideas with the
President. But, perhaps proving that direct access isn't all that
vital in the Nixon scheme of things, the President suddenly began
acting as Harlow and Buchanan, among others, had hoped he
would. He popped up at a Nevada State Society dinner in honor
of Pat Nixon and at a birthday party for retiring Republican
Senator Wallace Bennett of Utah. He invited the Republican
National Committee's coordinating committee to the White House
for breakfast and a 45-minute monologue and had in batches of
Republican senators and representatives for lengthy question-and-
answer sessions. Judging from the accounts that came out of the
closed meetings, the President assured his guests that he was going
to prove his innocence by telling all without telling them much
more than that he was going to tell all in other forums at other
times.

If the kind of disclosure that Mr. Nixon and his press secretary
practiced on November 12 is an indicator of what's to come, it
won't do the President the good he professes to believe it will. In
essence he could do no more than assert as his spokesmen previously had that two of nine White House tapes that he was under
court order to give federal Judge John Sirica were unavailable
because the conversations in question had not been recorded. He
also had to confess that a belt from a dictation machine, on which
he and his spokesmen had previously and repeatedly said he had
dictated his own account of one of the untaped conversations, was
not in the file where the President thought it was and therefore
could not be submitted to Judge Sirica. Mr. Nixon's dictated
recollection wouldn't have been worth much as evidence, at best,
but this latest claim that evidence once said to exist couldn't be
found knocked another hole in what remained of the President's
credibility. Press Secretary Ziegler was closer to open panic than
I've previously seen him when he begged reporters to "give us at

least a chance" and include the President's explanation in accounts of the dictation belt. An odd thing about that explanation is that the President didn't say he never dictated the account. He said only that the belt wasn't found where he'd thought it was. He left Ziegler to say it couldn't be found because it never existed.

November 24, 1973

XXXV

Slap, Tap, Pat?

Key Biscayne, Florida

When the President boarded Air Force One at a military base in northern Florida on the night of November 17, at the end of his fifth day on the counteroffensive against all those of little faith who were variously expecting and demanding his resignation or impeachment, he did something that he does only when he is pleased with himself and with the events that have preceded an embarkation. When he is displeased, he secludes himself in what his staff assumes to be both lone and sullen privacy. On this occasion, returning to his home on Key Biscayne from a hotel at Disney World, a beguiling enclave of commercialized fantasy near the city of Orlando, Mr. Nixon summoned the assistants who were traveling with him from their staff compartment to his compartment for a round of drinks and casual talk. He and the assistants agreed, and the public reaction by wire and telephone to the White House supported the happy estimate, that the President had done very well for himself during an hour and two minutes of televised answers to questions at a conference of newspaper editors.

One of the assistants, Patrick Buchanan, had prepared a briefing book of anticipated questions and possible answers and the President returned it to him with a note scrawled on the cover: "Buchanan—Many thanks! RN—11/17/73."

Morning and evening sessions at the White House with groups of congressional Republicans and with some 40 southern Democrats gave rise early in the week to a spate of stories to the general effect that the President was indeed meeting his Watergate problems and detractors "head on," as his spokesmen had said he would. His willingness to get out of Washington and around the country, though for starters only in a friendly section of the country, was demonstrated over the weekend and early the following week with visits to Disney World for the editors' conference; to Macon, Georgia, for a dual celebration of retired Congressman Carl T. Vinson's 90th birthday and the 100th anniversary of the law school at Mercer University, a rather obscure Baptist institution that Vinson attended; and to Memphis for a meeting with Republican governors who were assembled there and discussing, among other things, whether Mr. Nixon's leadership and the Watergate scandals had doomed the Republican Party to certain disaster in next year's mid-term elections.

Some interesting indications of Richard Nixon's problems and of how he and his people are trying to deal with them emerged from the Washington huddles and the southern travels. One of Mr. Nixon's problems is himself, and there were some discomforting signs during the southern foray that it's a substantial problem. His staff chief, General Alexander Haig, and his press secretary, Ronald Ziegler, made a special point of telling reporters on the presidential plane that their man's successive statements, in a speech on November 7 and in one of the answers at Disney World, that he is determined to carry on with his job "as long as I am physically able" signified absolutely nothing except that Mr. Nixon is working hard and thriving on the work. Ziegler realized, however, that the President's expressed preoccupation with his health was bound to arouse a certain wonderment about it, and he resolved to advise Mr. Nixon to get off that kick. Intermittently during his public performances, the President appeared to be tired and, at times, very tired. The familiar stoop of his shoulders and the droop of his mouth were more noticeable than usual and, in a few moments of extreme weariness, his whole face went slack and gray. The President's joking remark at the editors' conference that if his plane goes down "it goes down and then they don't have to impeach" was laughed at and applauded, but it seemed to me to be horribly unfunny. His habit of misusing words was much in evidence. In a feeble effort to get his question-answer duel with the editors off to a lightsome start, he said "answered" when he meant "asked" and "he" when he meant "I." The national television audience heard him thank a questioner for correcting his statement that his departed assistants, H. R. Haldeman and John Ehrlichman, "and others who have been charged are guilty until I have evidence that they are not guilty." Concentration upon such items as the foregoing enrages Mr. Nixon's assistants and spokesmen. They take it to be proof that the reporter guilty of it is gunning for the President and exaggerating behavior that, in anyone else, would go unnoticed. They have reason to believe and say this, sometimes. But there is a quality of exaggeration in their reaction to such reports that suggests a profoundly uneasy awareness on their part that their President is peculiarly vulnerable and is especially so when his fundamental stability under stress is brought into question. An episode that occurred at the Orlando airfield, after his session with the editors, brought the President's stability very much into question and elicited from the Nixon press staff a reaction that, in fierceness and sheer irrationality, was extraordinary even for that sensitive crew.

In the seven minutes that elapsed between the return of Mr. Nixon's party to the airfield and his jaunty run up the ramp of Air Force One, he showed that his grueling exchange with the editors had both elated and tired him. Usually, after a wearing appearance, he goes straight to his plane and departs, particularly when the only audience at his leaving is made up of service personnel and their dependents at air force bases like the one at Orlando. This time he shook hands with several people in the small crowd at the departure point and, just before he had his picture taken with a baby in his arms, exchanged a few words with a man and his son who turned out later to be Master Sergeant Edward

Kleizo and John Kleizo, aged seven. Two reporters, William J. Eaton of the *Chicago Daily News* and Matthew Cooney of the Westinghouse broadcast group, witnessed the encounter. They thought so little of its news value that they didn't mention it in a report they prepared that evening for the main Nixon press party. Sergeant Kleizo, off duty and in civvies, appeared to Eaton and Cooney, who were standing about five feet behind the President, to be a short, balding, pudgy man. The floodlights beating down upon the party seemed to bother Mr. Nixon in a way that they didn't Eaton and Cooney. The President said to Kleizo, "Are you the boy's mother or grandmother?" Kleizo said, "Neither." Mr. Nixon took a closer look and said to Kleizo, "Of course not." Eaton and Cooney then saw the President's right hand rise and touch Kleizo's face. Kleizo said to Eaton, "The President slapped me." Cooney heard John Kleizo saying, several times, "The President slapped my daddy." Fred Zimmerman, who covers the White House for the *Wall Street Journal,* got the story from Eaton and Cooney and devoted 81 words to it in the next edition of his paper. He said the President "soundly slapped" Kleizo. Other reporters picked up the story. Further inquiries and reflection pretty well established that it was a friendly slap, smart enough to be heard distinctly by Eaton and Cooney but, in Kleizo's account 48 hours later, understood by him to be a gesture of affection and apology for the President's initial error in thinking him a woman. That is the charitable and very possibly the correct interpretation of the incident. I'd accept it without quibble and I probably wouldn't have mentioned the absurd affair in this report, if the White House press staff had not erupted in the fashion now to be described.

A formal White House statement said: "Some members of the White House press corps, solely on the basis of rumor and gossip, distorted a friendly gesture in which the President patted a man on the face into a 'slapping incident.' The White House feels compelled to condemn this unethical and unprofessional reporting. This is an example of irresponsible and twisted accounts which have been circulated in recent months, without adequate substantiation and which create false impressions concerning the President of the United States. The motives of those who generated the rumors and those who wrote these stories can only be explained by the reporters involved." An "addendum," composed soon after the intial statement was perpetrated, said that "the White House press office expects" Zimmerman and James Deakin of the *St. Louis Post Dispatch,* one of several reporters who followed Zimmerman with accounts of the episode, "to correct the false impressions."

This seemingly trivial episode, which might appear to interest and concern only the journalists involved and to incline even them more to laughter than to outrage, actually calls for some comment. The stories did not arise from "rumor and gossip" but from an event that was observed by two reputable reporters. Almost certainly, the event was not the show of irrationality that it appeared to be but a gesture that, in its nature and because of the circumstances, lent itself to misinterpretation and was in fact misinterpreted at first. But the true and total irrationality is to be found in the White House reaction. To equate the slapping stories, most of which noted that maybe it was more of a smack or a pat than a slap, with the Watergate accounts over the past year that have put the President in a bad and generally deserved light, is to demonstrate a condition of paranoia and/or deliberate malignity more extreme than any that I have previously detected and reported at the Nixon White House.

It was indicated earlier in this report that several of Mr. Nixon's problems would be dealt with. Well, I'm out of space and overwhelmed with a feeling that the reaction to the stories about the slapping of Sergeant Kleizo says all that really needs to be said just now about the Nixon situation and establishment. The White House spokesman says formally and officially that "the President patted a man on the face." Fine. Let's stop right there.

December 1, 1973

———

The more I thought about the statement that "the White House press office expects" certain reporters and publications to do certain things, the angrier I became. At the first press briefing after the statement was issued, I asked Deputy Press Secretary Gerald Warren whether he and the President were aware of the similarity between that language and the language that came out of the Goebbels office in Hitler's time. Warren, obviously shaken and offended, said he rejected the thought implicit in my question.

XXXVI

At the Death

At times on November 26 and 27, listening to the testimony in federal Judge John J. Sirica's courtroom in Washington, I had a feeling that all of us there were sitting in at the death of the Nixon presidency. It was impossible to suppose at these times that Mr. Nixon could remain long in office or even want to if the offenses suggested by the circumstances that had led to this hearing and made all too believable by some of the testimony had in fact been committed in his behalf. For the circumstances were such that if the offenses had been committed at all, they would surely be judged in the public mind and very possibly be judged at criminal trials in this or other courts and by Congress in impeachment proceedings to have been committed in effect by the President himself.

The suggested and suspected offenses were perjury, obstruction of justice and, specifically, the deliberate obliteration of a portion of a White House tape recording. The tape recorded a conversation on June 20, 1972, three days after the Watergate break-in, between the President and H. R. Haldeman, who was then and

until last April 30 Mr. Nixon's staff chief. The obliteration of
18 minutes and 15 seconds of this tape was admitted by the
President's lawyers. The fact that the obliterated portion had
recorded a discussion of the Watergate affair was also admitted.
The questions in dispute and examination before Judge Sirica were
whether the erasure of the obliterated portion was deliberate or
accidental and whether the President's personal secretary, Rose
Mary Woods, lied under oath in this courtroom on November 8
and was lying again at this hearing. Her role was enough to identify
any offense that may have been committed in connection with the
June 20 tape closely and personally with the President. Rose Mary
Woods is a sort of Nixon institution. She has been the President's
secretary since 1951. He gave her the rank of executive assistant
to the President last June 12. It has been said of quite a few people around the President, notably Haldeman and John D. Ehrlichman, another assistant who resigned with Haldeman on April 30
because of association with the Watergate scandals, that they
would never have done anything in their official capacities that
they didn't know or believe the President wanted them to do.
This may be said more truly and certainly of Rose Mary Woods
than of anyone else in the President's past or present employ.
If she lied, he lied. If she tampered with the June 20 tape or any
other Watergate tape, he did. One must add, "in effect." It's a
pro forma addition, for the record only.

The central questions at issue before Judge Sirica on November
8 and afterward were questions of presidential guilt or innocence.
But, in this situation as in all of the other Watergate situations,
a question of competence was also at issue. As these reports have
previously noted, one of Mr. Nixon's difficulties is that his claims
of innocence can be credited only if extreme and pervasive incompetence at the Nixon White House is assumed and recognized.
Nothing demonstrates the truth of this assertion more thoroughly
than the story of the erasure of the June 20 tape. Here is the
essence of the story as the President, his attorneys and Rose Mary
Woods tell it.

Mr. Nixon said in a statement on November 12 that he concluded in "late September" that he should turn over "the full
substance" of White House recordings of 10 of his conversations

to the Senate Watergate committee and to Judge Sirica for a federal grand jury. The President's declared intention until late September to withhold all of the White House tapes from outside scrutiny could have explained, at least in part, the glaring carelessness and stupidity with which the tapes were handled both before and after their existence was revealed in July. That excuse vanished when Mr. Nixon decided to allow some disclosure. Everything that has happened in connection with the tapes since September must be evaluated on the assumption that the President is telling the truth when he says he has known since then that the substance if not the precise and total content of some of them would become known.

One of the first things that happened was that recordings of three of the 10 conversations could not be found. At least five months had passed since the President developed enough concern about the tapes to have some of them reviewed for him and four months had passed since he listened to a batch of them. A frantic search turned up one of the missing three recordings. Its discovery contributed to a hope that the other two might also be found and—so I was told at the time—accounted for the fact that the search was not abandoned until October 27. This bit about finding one of three recordings and consequently prolonging the search for the other two seemed to me to be pretty convincing. Although it might have helped to dispel the doubts and shock that inevitably arose when Judge Sirica and the public were told on October 31 that two of the 10 conversations were never recorded, it was not exploited or even mentioned by the President's spokesmen. So far as I know, it is reported here for the first time.

The June 20 tape was among eight recordings that were given to Rose Mary Woods for transcription and summary, in preparation for any degree of disclosure the President finally decided upon. A subpoena issued by former Special Prosecutor Archibald Cox on July 23 and a supporting memorandum filed with the US Court of Appeals in the District of Columbia on August 13 make it clear beyond question, to any moderately perceptive reader of both documents, that the entire recording of the President's meetings on June 20 with John Ehrlichman and Bob Haldeman was called for. The language of the documents is imprecise and the subpoena refers to one meeting instead of the two successive meetings, first with Ehrlichman and then with Haldeman, that actually occurred. But the intent is unmistakable. Yet J. Fred Buzhardt, a White House lawyer who has been handling Watergate and tape problems for the President since last May, indicated in a written report to Judge Sirica and testified explicitly that he thought until November 14, and advised the President, that the subpoena and subsequent court orders called only for the Ehrlichman portion of the June 20 tape. Buzhardt said he didn't get around to serious study of the August 13 memorandum, which should have corrected any doubt raised by the subpoena, until November 14 and realized only then that both the Ehrlichman and Haldeman portions of the tape were subpoenaed.

An interesting thing about this assertion of abysmal neglect and error is that it was essential to the story that Rose Mary Woods told under oath on November 26–27. Her hope of escaping indictment for perjury rested importantly on her and Buzhardt's contention that on November 8, when she testified in support of the President's story that two subpoenaed recordings could not be produced because they had never existed, the understanding at the White House was that the Haldeman segment of the June 20 tape had not been subpoenaed. The same contention has to be believed if the White House story of the President's indifference to the obliteration of part of the Haldeman portion of the tape is believed. The story is that Miss Woods told him on October 1 that she had accidentally blanked out four to five minutes of the Haldeman segment and that he told her not to worry about it because that part of the tape was not subpoenaed. On November 20, five days after he is said to have been told by Buzhardt that the erasure was much more extensive than had first been supposed and also that it occurred in a subpoenaed part of the tape, Mr. Nixon didn't think the impending disclosure worth mentioning to a group of Republican governors in Memphis. He told them that he didn't expect any more Watergate shocks. The erasure was reported to Judge Sirica and announced the next day.

There were significant differences between the stories that Miss Woods and Buzhardt told Judge Sirica and between the stories that Buzhardt told the judge in two written statements and then in testimony. Miss Woods refused to admit that she'd erased anything. She stuck throughout to her story that she'd accidentally and simultaneously pushed down the "record" button on a tape transcriber she was using on October 1 and kept the tape running on "record" with a foot pedal while she answered a telephone call that she thought must have continued for between four and five minutes. She acknowledged that this "caused a gap" and imposed a high-frequency hum on something like five minutes of the tape. She said she hadn't listened to the portion with the gap and therefore didn't know that there had been any conversation on it to be erased. Eighteen minutes and 15 seconds of the tape actually had the hum and no audible words on it. This segment was preceded and followed by audible conversation between Haldeman and the President, including Haldeman's remark that he wondered whether anybody read *The New Republic*. All of the other remarks played back in court were about as inane as this one. Miss Woods said again and again that she could not have blanked out 18 minutes of the tape, a claim that perhaps improved her shaky position but didn't improve the White House position. Judge Sirica, listening with discernible skepticism to this and much more from Miss Woods, was less interested in the difference between maybe five and 18 minutes of wordless hum than he was in Miss Woods' failure to mention what she now called "a terrible mistake" when she testified on November 8. He asked her why she hadn't mentioned it and instead had sworn that she hadn't altered any tapes in any way. She answered that she thought on November 8 that only the subpoenaed tapes were being discussed and she had the President's assurance at that time that the Haldeman portion wasn't subpoenaed.

Buzhardt said in a statement on November 21 that White House lawyers hadn't found out what caused the hum. He said in a report to Judge Sirica on November 26 that it "was caused by the depression of a record button during the process of reviewing the tape, possibly while the recorder was in the proximity of an electric typewriter and a high intensity lamp." An IBM electric typewriter and a high intensity lamp were on Miss Woods' desk at the White House on October 1, when she says she made her "terrible mistake." She wasn't mentioned in the November 26 report to the judge, but the effect of it was to say that she had in fact caused the entire 18-minute hum and blank-out. Buzhardt and Leonard Garment, the acting White House counsel, were considerably more explicit when they reported the matter first to the new special prosecutor, Leon Jaworski, and then to Judge Sirica in private on November 21. They told Jaworski and Sirica that Miss Woods had done it; that they were not certain whether it was done accidentally or on purpose; that, on the basis of tests so far conducted, it was hard to see how it could have been done accidentally; and that, in the circumstances, she would have to be represented by her own lawyer rather than by White House attorneys when she was called to testify. With obvious but controlled resentment, Miss Woods said during her testimony that General Alexander Haig, the President's chief of staff, told her on the evening of the 21st that she'd have to retain a lawyer of her own. She said Haig called Charles Rhyne, a distinguished Washington attorney and longtime friend of the President, and arranged for him to represent her. She indicated but didn't quite say that her friend and employer of 22 years, the President, avoided any contact and discussion with her at this stage.

A rather odd facet of the White House posture, as distinct from that of Rose Mary Woods, was that the President's staff attorneys didn't know when they first reported to Judge Sirica, and didn't mention in court when they came to know, that an 18-minute erasure on the transcriber used by Miss Woods could very easily have occurred by accident. A professional electronics man with knowledge of that particular machine told me that it could have happened, and if it did would have produced the exact hum that was heard in court, if Miss Woods had touched the fast rewind control on her foot pedal for just a few seconds while the recorder button was down. Miss Woods said, rather indignantly, that she didn't make *that* mistake. But the supposition that she did is much more plausible than her story and Buzhardt's story that the recorder's proximity to her typewriter and tensor lamp could have caused the hum. My man said that the typewriter motor or the lamp might have caused a hum, but not that kind of high and rasping hum. There were two separate White House tests with the transcriber beside the typewriter and lamp. One of the tests produced a hum. One did not.

December 8, 1973

――――――

My expert's explanation of how the gap and hum could have been caused proved to be highly doubtful. A court-appointed panel found that the gap was caused by manual erasures. This was further disputed by a White House expert who, according to Nixon officials, said it could have been and probably was caused by a defect in Miss Woods' recorder.

XXXVII

Ford on Ford

The chairmen and members of the Senate and House committees that approved the nomination of Congressman Gerald Ford to be the next Vice President of the United States spoke often at the hearings on the nomination as if they expected Ford to replace Richard Nixon in the presidency and were deciding whether he is fit to do so. They never said this. But there was in their comments something more and deeper than orthodox expressions of awareness that Presidents are mortal and that any Vice President may succeed his President. Whether Mr. Nixon will finish out his second term or will resign, be impeached and removed, or be declared incompetent to conduct the office while still in it is a subject of speculation and argument in Congress as it is throughout the country. Chairman Howard Cannon said that his Senate Rules Committee "should view its obligations as no less important than the selection of a potential President of the United States." Chairman Peter Rodino said at the start of the House Judiciary Committee's hearings that "what we may indeed be undertaking this morning is an examination of a man's qualifications and fit-ness to hold the highest office in America, that of President of the United States." Congressman Ford, testifying before the committees, rarely bothered with conventional quibbles to the effect that he didn't expect to be anything other than a Vice President and answered matter of factly when he was asked what he'd do "if you were President." For a minor example, he said that he had advised Mr. Nixon to have press conferences "more frequently than he has" and indicated that if he were President he'd plan to hold them "every other week at the least."

Believing what politicians say about themselves is not in fashion. Ford in his testimony of course was saying what he thought it expedient and prudent to say in the interest of getting his nomination confirmed with a minimum of trouble and opposition. But what he thought it expedient and prudent to say in these unique circumstances, the first when an incumbent President nominated a Vice President and Congress had to approve or disapprove the nomination by majority vote in both houses, told a good deal that's worth noting and remembering about Gerald Ford now that he is Vice President Ford.

Ford said his main reason for considering himself qualified to be Vice President is that "I believe I can be a ready conciliator and calm communicator between the White House and Capitol Hill, between the reelection mandate of the Republican President and the equally emphatic mandate of the Democratic 93rd Congress." A reason for believing this, he said, is that he has come to know the Congress well during 25 years as a member of the House of Representatives from Michigan and eight years as the Republican minority leader in the House. White House Counsellor and former Congressman Melvin Laird, whose chief assignment of late has been to get Ford confirmed and has said he's quitting the Nixon staff as soon as the Vice President has settled in, has also said that he expects Vice President Ford to be the President's principal advocate and most effective lobbyist on Capitol Hill. Ford indicated in different answers that he did and didn't think this a realistic view. Senators Lyndon Johnson, Hubert Humphrey and Alben Barkley discovered in recent times that their clout with the Senate melted away when they became Vice Presidents.

Ford's disgraced predecessor, Spiro T. Agnew, never recovered from the harm he did himself during his first months in the vice presidency when he presumed to tell senators how to vote. When Senator James B. Allen of Alabama asked in effect whether he'd be a presidential lobbyist or "an impartial presiding officer of the Senate," Ford answered: ". . . I would, without any doubt, be an impartial presiding officer. I think that is mandatory. I do not think I ought to say I would be a crusader in the ranks on any issue, as far as the President's policy is concerned. If somebody asked me my views, I would certainly express them. If I am asked to try and work out compromises during the legislative process, I certainly would be available and contribute my input. But I would not talk to individual senators like I now have the responsibility of talking to individual House members." He told the House committee that "I certainly hope to spend a substantial amount of my time in the US Senate as the presiding officer. I do expect, however, that I will be doing some work while I am on Capitol Hill, trying to get legislation through a Democratic Congress with a Republican President. I think I can contribute effectively in that way."

Ford said he couldn't imagine why people keep asking him whether he supports President Nixon on particular items and in general. He said his answer is: "Of course I support the President. He is my friend of a quarter century. His political philosophy is very close to my own. He is the head of my party and the constitutional chief executive of the nation. He was chosen quite emphatically by the people a year ago as I, if confirmed as Vice President, will not have been." He added that he nevertheless is his own man; that he's opposed this Republican President and Democratic Presidents "when I thought they were wrong"; and then said: "To be honest, I imagine that as Vice President you do your presidential criticizing a little more privately than publicly." In an exchange with Congressman Charles E. Wiggins of California on November 15, Ford said he had met with the President "roughly 15 times" since he was nominated on October 12. He said that General Alexander Haig, the President's staff chief, called him on "three or four" of these occasions and asked him to see the President. On several occasions, he continued, "I called

General Haig and asked to see the President." On several other occasions "I and others had met with the President and I stayed longer than they, and on those occasions I had no intercession by anybody." Wiggins said he hoped that Ford as Vice President wouldn't "feel it is necessary to clear your meetings with General Haig or with anyone" and concluded: "You have a right to talk to the President, it seems to me, and face him directly and personally." Ford replied: "I have found no problems whatsoever thus far in getting to see the President. As a matter of fact he has shown great interest in talking to me about matters which I appreciate because I think it is indicative that he wants whatever information or advice I can give and I can assure you that, if confirmed, I hope that that personal relationship . . . will be expanded."

Congressman Henry P. Smith III of New York reminded Ford that "the possibility is always there that you might be President of the United States" and asked him to describe his "background in foreign affairs." Ford replied: "I think being a member of the US Congress for 25 years, in the House, one does acquire considerable background in the field of foreign affairs." He said his membership on three Appropriations subcommittees dealing with defense, foreign aid and CIA matters "was extremely helpful and beneficial" and provided travel "in Europe, in Asia, in other parts of the world." These memberships ended when he became minority leader in 1965. He recalled his attendance at Interparliamentary Union meetings in Warsaw, Belgrade and Brussels. Also: "I have been privileged to attend a number of meetings at the White House under various Presidents where matters involving foreign policy were discussed and programs were executed or implemented [sic]." And—a point he made whenever his shortage of foreign policy experience came up—a 12-day visit to mainland China last year gave him and the late Hale Boggs of Louisiana "a unique opportunity to travel the length and breadth of China and to meet extensively with top leaders of the People's Republic of China." All of this, he thought, gave him "a background that is at least equal to my predecessors in the office of Vice President." When he was asked, "If the mantle of the presidency fell upon you, would it be your intention to keep Dr. Kissinger as Secretary of

State?" Ford answered: "I think he is a superb Secretary of State."

Jacob Javits of New York, a Republican senator with maverick tendencies, said on December 5 that the pressures upon President Nixon to resign were certain to increase once a Republican Vice President and available successor was again in office. This factor, the prospect of a prolonged pre-impeachment inquiry by the House Judiciary Committee, and the visible fact that Mr. Nixon isn't looking well in some of his public appearances, justify a suggestion that citizens acquaint themselves with sections 3 and 4 of the 25th Amendment to the Constitution. Sections 1 and 2 provide that the Vice President shall succeed the President in event of removal, death or resignation, and that a vacancy in the vice presidency shall be filled in the way the vacancy left by Spiro Agnew was filled. Sections 3 and 4 deal with what happens when a President reports himself or is found to be "unable to discharge the powers and duties of his office." In that event, "such powers and duties shall be discharged by the Vice President as Acting President."

December 15, 1973

XXXVIII

Pay No More

In the federal income tax returns that the President made public on December 8, as part of what he called "a full disclosure of my financial affairs," there were three deductions for "depreciation of personally owned White House furniture." They reduced Mr. Nixon's taxable income by $1347.36 in 1970, $1094.73 in 1971, and $889.47 in 1972. By comparison with the items that produced deductions totaling $988,963.43 from a gross income of $1,122,-266.39 in the four years 1969–72, the furniture deductions were trivial. But they and some other relatively minor elements of the President's tax history seem to me to tell more than the big items do about the attitudes and practices that brought Richard Nixon to the point of assuring the nation at a televised press conference on November 17 that "I am not a crook" and of trying to prove that he isn't with his "full disclosure."

One of the pieces of depreciated furniture is the Cabinet table in the Cabinet Room next to the President's Oval Office in the West Wing of the White House. It's a magnificent object, done in oak and leather. Mr. Nixon, dissatisfied with the table in use when he was inaugurated, ordered a new table in March of 1969 and paid $4816.84 for it. He said when he did this that he would give the table to the nation when he left the presidency. In the meantime it's been his property, legally subject to the annually diminishing charge for depreciation that his tax accountant, Arthur Blech of Los Angeles, has claimed on his behalf. The second of two depreciated items is a set of office furniture, and a ludicrous story is connected with it. As of December 11, the White House assistants working on the disclosure process didn't know where this furniture was, what it included, or why it was bought. One of the assistants said it could be in the West Wing, across the street in the Executive Office Building, or in presidential office quarters in San Clemente or Key Biscayne. "The truth is," this assistant said, "nobody has gone to the President and asked him about it." Translated, this meant that nobody had dared to ask the President about it. All that the assistants knew about the set of furniture was that it included a desk and that the Pavlov Office Furniture Co., address undetermined, was paid for it in July of 1969 with a check for $2369.12. Although the matter didn't come up at the six press briefings held on December 7 and 8 in connection with the financial disclosure, a spokesman said that the deducted total of $3331.56 in three years on furniture that cost a total of $7185.96 was legal and proper. It was indicated that further deductions could and presumably would be taken.

One of the President's three real estate properties is the Whittier, California, home that his mother, Hannah Nixon, owned and occupied when she died. The 1969–72 returns show rental income from this property of $2400.05 and deducted expenses totaling $26,470.87 over the four years. Its evident use as a tax haven caused some close questioning at the press briefings. Arthur Blech, the Los Angeles accountant, said that two Internal Revenue Service agents spent more time—one-and-a-half hours—on this item than on any other when they audited the President's 1971–72 returns last May. Blech said the Whittier data satisfied the agents. He also said that "it is a question of a very valuable piece of land worth about $90,000 with a building on it worth $8000. The building is old, dilapidated, very bad, in disrepair." Newspaper and television pictures showed a two-story, stucco house that seemed to be in decent shape. It generally rents for $50 per month and the annual income has varied from $700 in 1969 to $450 in 1972. The tenant since October 1972 has been the East Whittier Friends Church (Quaker), to which the President gave $250 in 1969 and $100 in 1971. These are among the charitable contributions totaling $13,481 over four years and varying from $7512 in 1971 to $295 in 1972 that are reported and deducted on the 1969–72 returns. One of the church's two ministers, the Reverend Charles Mylander, and his family live in the house and did not appreciate the accountant's description of it. In 1969, a typical year, the deducted Whittier loss of $5699.16 included $818.60 in depreciation, $68 for insurance, $1895.65 in property taxes, and the largest item, $3257.14 in interest on a mortgage on the property. Nothing was charged off for maintenance of the house, though a $290 item is marked "clean up."

An intriguing glimpse of Mr. Nixon in one of his personal aspects and of his staff relationships is provided by the references during the disclosure operation to his acquisition in 1967 and sale in early 1969 of 185,891 shares of stock in Fisher's Island, Inc., a Miami development company formed and controlled by a group of Nixon friends who include Charles G. (Bebe) Rebozo. Reams of rumor and established fact have been printed, much of it unflattering to the President and his associates in this deal and some of it suggesting that Rebozo arranged for Mr. Nixon to be paid much more for his stock than it was worth. That is not the principal point of interest here. Mr. Nixon bought 199,891 Fisher shares at $1 a share and sold all but 14,000 shares of his holding back to the Fisher's Island company for $2 a share. He declared a capital gain of $184,891 in his 1969 return and some of the $72,682.09 that he paid in 1969 income tax was on this gain. It was disclosed on December 8 that three people who worked for Mr. Nixon in 1967 and still work with him took options on the 14,000 shares at $1 per share when he bought his Fisher's Island stock in 1967. His personal secretary, Rose Mary Woods, took 10,000 shares. His valet, Manolo Sanchez, took 1000 shares. Patrick Buchanan, a speechwriter and consulting thinker, took 3000 shares. Miss Woods and Sanchez exercised their options in early 1969 and immediately sold their shares back to the company at $2 a share when Mr. Nixon sold his. How Miss Woods and Sanchez financed their 1967 options was not explained. Buchanan told me how he did. He loaned Mr. Nixon $3000 on the understanding, backed up with a demand note, that six percent interest would be paid when and if the loan was repaid in cash. Buchanan says this was an actual loan, with $3000 passing from him to Mr. Nixon. The President has said that he was earning $100,000 to $250,000 a year with his New York law firm at the time. Buchanan picked up his 3000 optioned shares in 1969 when Mr. Nixon, Sanchez and Miss Woods were selling their shares. Buchanan says that he was paid no interest and kept his shares because he thought it was a good investment. The Fisher's Island company has offered additional shares at $1 per share since 1969 and Buchanan has bought 820 more at $1. This fact indicates that Mr. Nixon, Miss Woods and Sanchez got extremely good deals when they sold their shares at $2.

These minor chapters in the big Nixon story bring to mind a couple of other small stories about the President. They didn't emerge during the disclosure orgy but are relevant to it. A White House assistant recalls reading a memorandum that the President wrote early in his first term to John D. Ehrlichman, then his staff counsel in charge of his personal affairs. The assistant says that the memorandum went into much detail about how the President wanted his $200,000 salary, his $50,000 annual expense allowance—actually a part of his remuneration, subject to income tax to the extent that it isn't spent on official business—and his other income and assets handled. According to the assistant, who by definition is biased toward Mr. Nixon, it was not the instruction of a man who had anything to hide or who was conscious of doing anything wrong. It was the memorandum of a fairly wealthy man who cared intensely about his money, his family and his heirs, and who wanted his taxes held to the absolute minimum that they could be legally held to. It was the work of a lawyer who was versed in the late Judge Learned Hand's dictum that nobody is obligated to pay more taxes than the law requires and who interprets this unexceptional doctrine to mean that he and his accountants are entitled to the very last deduction that they can think up or discover. Perhaps the most fascinating item in Mr.

Nixon's 1969–72 returns is the deduction of $1.24 in interest on a department store charge. In that year, 1971, the President reported $262,384.75 in gross income, claimed $255,676.69 in deductions, and paid $878.03 in federal tax on a reported taxable income of $5358.06.

The second story is told by a southern Republican lawyer who visited Mr. Nixon at his New York apartment in 1968, before he was nominated. Mr. Nixon said he assumed that the lawyer was visiting New York on clients' business and would charge the trip to them or, at the very least, would deduct the charge on his tax returns as a business expense. The visiting lawyer said he probably wouldn't; it really was a personal trip. Mr. Nixon looked as if he were shocked, made the visitor repeat that he did have some clients in New York, and finally extracted an admission that his visitor could, if he worked at it, concoct a passable excuse for either a charge to clients or a tax deduction. Mr. Nixon cocked his right thumb and forefinger at the visitor, winked, and made a *chucking* sound. The visiting lawyer, telling this story to a partner who told it to me, said he found the episode embarrassing and never afterward had much respect for Richard Nixon.

An IRS audit of the President's 1971–72 tax returns and the fact that it resulted from a random selection of high income and low tax returns became known during the disclosure exercise. It was not officially revealed, but it is a fact, that Internal Revenue Commissioner Johnnie Walters, who has left office since the audit was ordered, was shaken and uncertain when a computer turned up the President's 1972 return last spring. Walters telephoned a White House assistant and asked him what should be done. The assistant asked whether the law or regulations required the audit of returns selected at random as the President's was. Walters said an audit was indeed required. Without checking with the President, the assistant told Walters to proceed with the audit. It appears from the December 8 account that the 1971 return was also audited. The significance of this addition to the official story is that a President's tax returns get special attention but not necessarily special and favored treatment at IRS. This shouldn't surprise anyone.

Mr. Nixon has asked the joint Senate-House Committee on Internal Revenue Taxation to pass upon the legality and propriety of the tax action that worries him most. A $576,000 deduction that he took upon the gift of his vice presidential papers to the national archives in 1969 reduced his taxable income over 1969–72 by $482,019 and reduced the income taxes that he otherwise would have owed by some $234,000. The transaction is open to question on several grounds, among them a shortage of documentation of the claim that the gift was effectively made before a 1969 law invalidated such deductions. The uncertainty of the President's spokesmen about the outcome of this controversy is evident from their strident insistence that Mr. Nixon's intention to give the nation the papers is clear and that the rest is mere technicality. The rest could involve serious falsifications of fact. But Mr. Nixon has had to take a bum rap on one score. His derided story that Lyndon Johnson put him up to the papers dodge is inaccurate in detail but believable in substance. Mr. Johnson took all the tax deductions he could get from gifts of his vice presidential papers and was profanely and extremely aggravated when the 1969 law did him out of a deduction far greater than the ones Mr. Nixon claimed on his 1968 and subsequent incomes. The law did Mr. Johnson out of it, that is to say, because he was wise enough to take some advice that Mr. Nixon either didn't get or ignored. Sheldon Cohen, who was internal revenue commissioner in the Johnson time, told Mr. Johnson that he could beat the deadline if he insisted but would be foolish to try it. Mr. Nixon tried it and is in trouble. The President who signed that 1969 law, incidentally, was Richard Nixon.

December 22, 1973

XXXIX

A Bad Year

Here is how it was at a few points and with a few people around the White House toward the end of the first year of Richard Nixon's second term, a year that promised to be a time of accomplishment and triumph and seems likely at this writing to be the last full year of the Nixon presidency.

John K. Andrews, Jr., a young writer of presidential statements who quit in early December after four years on the Nixon staff, left a farewell missive that he entitled "Memorandum for an honorable company of friends from a departing scrivener." Because of what it says and reflects, the memorandum is more important than its author was at the White House. Andrews is a quiet sort, intense and reserved, a Christian Scientist, a true believer. At the White House he avoided reporters, partly (I gathered) because they tend not to be true believers. He appeared to resent their cavalier attitudes toward the President. I once read a confidential account of a meeting between Mr. Nixon and some visiting admirers that Andrews had written "for the President's file" and I thought it repellently slavish. Andrews discussed with a few friends on the staff his reasons for quitting and what he should and shouldn't say in his goodbye screed. He made it starkly plain to them that he'd finally had more than he could take of Watergate and all that it signified. In late 1973, he told them, things got to the point where it was difficult for him to put his heart in the work anymore. Behind this simple and common disillusionment was a mix of feelings and motives that perhaps can be fully credible only to people who have worked for Richard Nixon and have committed themselves to him as completely as John Andrews had. It is difficult, close to impossible, for believers such as Andrews to conclude that their trust has been totally misplaced. He and a good many others at the White House clung to a notion that their President could exonerate himself if he had the wit to do it and, therefore, that his fault was a matter of ineptitude and not of guilt. In anguished conversations with his friends, Andrews maintained that the President could have moved more effectively than he had to clear himself and that his failure to do so had unnecessarily damaged him, his presidency and the country. It was this failure, Andrews indicated, that he could no longer tolerate and forgive.

Some of the foregoing was intimated but none of it was stated in the Andrews memorandum. Andrews omitted overt strictures because he didn't want to aid and comfort those who, in his view, were taking advantage of Watergate and its associations to tear down Richard Nixon. What Andrews omitted makes what he chose to say more interesting. Before quoting the references to Mr. Nixon and his situation, however, I quote a passage that documents a rarely documented point about the Nixon White House. It is staffed in part by people who have the same sense of religious mission that John Andrews has, whatever their formal religion may be, and who truly believe (or have believed) that in serving Mr. Nixon they serve a cause that is at once righteous and bigger than themselves. As the President has suggested, one of the consequences is a fervor that may do more than any theory of simple villainy to explain some of the Watergate excesses. After noting that he was about to move to Denver and "become Director of Communications for Adventure Unlimited, an organization which conducts a Christian youth ministry in this country and abroad,"

Andrews told his White House colleagues: "This perhaps is not as sharp a career turn as it looks since it seems to me, as Senator Hughes has put it, that a prime means of improving government and society is to strengthen individuals' spiritual reliance. So we'll still be on parallel paths and I hope to keep in touch." His reference to Senator Hughes is to Harold Hughes of Iowa, who is leaving politics for Christian labor. Adventure Unlimited is a Christian Science endeavor and Andrews' father is its chairman.

The righteousness, the self-pity, the apprehension and the desperate need to believe themselves to be honorable servants of an honorable leader that are evident among Nixon assistants after 18 months of the Watergate horror throb out from the Andrews memorandum. Its central portion follows: "The President recently likened himself to a ship captain in stormy seas, and an admirably brave one he is. Carrying out the metaphor, I'd only say that he's damn fortunate to sail with a crew with as much dedication and principle and grit as you on the staff have shown even in heaviest weather. Up ahead, the steadiest star that I can see to steer by is our own 1968 statement [in a Nixon speech, though Andrews didn't say so] that the Presidency is preeminently a place of moral leadership. Held to that course, this Administration, which has already brought the nation and the world so far with often so little thanks, cannot fail to make safe port. Great endeavors risk great errors, as we have learned to our pain; but the forces they loose are certain to unmake the unworthy and only deepen character in the best. In that confidence, I am of good cheer and full of hope for America." The recipients noticed that the expression of hope for America was not accompanied by a similar expression of hope for Mr. Nixon.

Other departures are imminent; some of them have been announced; and all of them have been or will be interpreted as rejections of Mr. Nixon, flights from association with him, or both. In the few instances of impending departures known to me but not announced, this interpretation is incorrect. It is possible, after all, for good people to get tired of working in one place for five years and to want a change. Raymond Price and Lee Huebner among the President's staff writers, and Richard Fairbanks on the

Domestic Council staff, intend to get out when they can do so
with no or minimal damage to the President. Former Congressman
and Defense Secretary Melvin Laird, who said when he became a
counsellor to the President last June that he'd stay for "at least
a year," made it official that he's quitting as of February 1. Lack-
ing any factual basis for doubting that Laird has been as useful
to the President as he (Laird) claims to have been, particularly
with legislation and the nomination and confirmation of Vice President Gerald Ford, I note the claim and observe that Mr. Nixon
cannot be overcome with sorrow. Laird, bent upon magnifying
his own importance, let it be known months ago that the President didn't really like him or want him around and tolerated his
advent only because powerful Republicans insisted on it.

It's disgraceful of me to deal with such petty factors in a time
of stress and torment, but I can't resist reference to a couple of
other comical aspects of Laird's brief tenure at the White House.
He and Henry Kissinger hate each other's guts. Kissinger, who
hadn't been appointed Secretary of State when Laird joined the
Nixon staff, correctly assumed that Laird would insist on being
made a member of the National Security Council and would do
what he could to diminish Kissinger's preeminence in foreign affairs. That turned out to be very little, Laird's foreign policy responsibilities being mostly figments of his yearning, and Kissinger
soon sealing his supremacy with his dual status as assistant for
national security affairs and Secretary of State. The other relationship in mind here is Laird's with Bryce Harlow, who has been in
and out of Republican White Houses since the 1950s and, in his
intervals of private employment, represents Procter & Gamble in
Washington. Harlow, who returned to the Nixon staff last summer
on a Watergate rescue mission, and Laird frequently insult each
other in terms that cannot be provably shown to be intentional
insults. Laird, for instance, seemed to be aglow with affection for a
cherished friend when he was asked on December 19 about reports
that Harlow is leaving the staff and replied that "every time Bryce
Harlow has come to the White House, he has always been leaving
and he has always established that the first day he got here." It's
true, but it's not the kind of thing that a friend says about a friend
at a press conference.

Bryce Harlow's story that he's intended since last summer to leave the Nixon service around this time doesn't wash. What he's previously said, to my knowledge, has been that he'd go back to Procter & Gamble and to the large amounts of money that he is reported to earn there when his presence at the White House is no longer considered to be indispensable. Harlow speaks of indispensability in a tone of wry deprecation that acquits him of unacceptable vanity. If he is in fact considered to be dispensable, one of two conclusions is indicated. Harlow may have concluded that Richard Nixon is beyond saving. Or Mr. Nixon may have settled upon a course known to Harlow and to very few others that makes it unnecessary for Harlow to stay around much longer. What I'm saying, with no support except fallible intuition, is that Harlow may know, sense or suspect with overwhelming force that Richard Nixon has decided to resign when and if he judges that the alternatives to resignation are impeachment by the House of Representatives and conviction by the Senate.

Despite their reputation for influence with Congress—a reputation that Harlow has the grace to laugh at—both of the departing staff counsellors must know that they and any arguments that they may offer will have little or nothing to do with the outcome of the impeachment process. The outcome will depend upon the revealed facts and, more importantly, upon the public's perception of the facts. The massive disclosure on December 8 of statistics and assertions bearing upon the President's tax history and financial resources proved to be a crushing disappointment to his associates and presumably to him. Instead of quieting the questions and cynicism, the disclosure fed them. Before the negative impact of the December 8 exercise sank in, White House reporters were told to expect further disclosures. There were to be transcripts of subpoenaed Watergate tapes; White House data concerning the dairy industry and the benefits it got from the Nixon administration; documents related to the International Telephone and Telegraph Corporation and the breaks it got in antitrust litigation; and facts about the domestic surveillance operation that the President initiated in 1970. A hiatus occurred. There were no further disclosures, when they were intended and unofficially promised, before Congress took its Christmas recess and prepared for the prospective horrors of 1974.

The President's spokesman said during the week before Christ-

mas that he wanted to go to Florida for a few days of warmth and
rest but hadn't decided whether and when and how he'd go. The
bind on him was the energy crisis. His choice was a train or a small
jet or Air Force One, the Boeing 707 jet that he usually rides. The
choice was tightened upon him by White House reporters who got
what they asked for when they raised questions about the jet fuel
(2800 gallons, and so what?) that the President's plane consumes
on a flight from Washington to Miami. I'm told and believe that
it was at Mr. Nixon's instance that his spokesman said okay—no
Air Force One for the President, no press plane chartered by the
White House transportation staff. No hotel rooms reserved for the
press by the transportation staff. No hire-cars reserved for the press
by the same staff. Climactically and with special vengeance, no
"pools" of reporters and photographers would hereafter accompany
the President on trips to his Florida and California homes. The
employers of the reporters, cameramen and assorted electronic
technicians who travel with the President pay at first-class rates
for the accommodations arranged by the transportation staff.
Somebody, presumably the involved head of household, pays at
cut rates for the transportation on the Florida and California trips
of hordes of spouses and squalling offspring. I've long thought this
to be a damnable imposition on writing journalists who are compelled to travel in the airborne hell of the coach sections unless
they outrace the cameramen and technicians, a remarkably successful breed of seat-grabbers, to the few first-class seats. The point
here is not the trivial intraprofessional rivalry and the misogynistic
sentiments so far indicated, for which I offer no apology. The point
is that the media and media employees, beginning with but not
confined to the 100 or so souls who style themselves "White House
regulars," have demanded and accepted help and favors from
successive White House regimes that shouldn't be demanded. The
current reminder, probably induced by the meanest motives, that
the favors are not grounded in the constitution and are subject to
withdrawal ought in my opinion to be welcomed.

Somewhere back in this report, I said it was disgraceful of me
to deal with petty matters. I promised my editors and they promised in the previous issue of this journal that I'd be reviewing Mr.
Nixon's bad year. Well, what in God's name is there to say except

that 1973 was a bad year? The little that I hear from people and the much that I hear on television and radio and read in newspapers tells me that there is nothing—absolutely nothing—that I can add to the general perception of Mr. Nixon. Except this—presumably and fantastically addressed to people who don't read *The New Republic.* You voted for him. Unlike the editors of this journal, I'd have voted for him, too, over George McGovern, if I hadn't just got off a Nixon press plane when the polls were about to close and been busy writing that we had voted ourselves four more years of Richard Nixon. In my opinion, the impeachment process was not intended by the framers of the constitution and shouldn't be used to correct the errors of the electorate, absent the most compelling evidence that the President is a felon. Friends say, Who would you vote for today, Nixon or McGovern? It is an idle question. The relevant question now is, Nixon or Gerald Ford? I'll take Ford.

January 5–12, 1974

———

Rose Mary Woods, the President's confidential secretary and executive assistant, asked Harlow whether he had given me the notion that something he knew or sensed about Mr. Nixon's intentions affected Harlow's own intention to resign. She was told the notion didn't come from Harlow, and he convinced me that it was erroneous. The President persuaded him to stay awhile longer than he'd intended. Both Laird and Harlow told me, and I am compelled against my gut judgment to believe, that Harlow put Laird up to the crack about always leaving.

Index

ABOUT THE AUTHOR

John Osborne was born in Corinth, Mississippi, in 1907. During forty-seven years in journalism, beginning with southern newspapers and The Associated Press, he has been *Newsweek*'s labor specialist and national editor; labor, military and foreign affairs writer and foreign editor of *Time;* staff writer, foreign editor and chief editorial writer of *Life;* chief of the Time-Life London bureau and senior Time-Life correspondent in the Far East; and a contributor to *Fortune*. He is author of two Time-Life books— *Britain: A Country of Character* and *The Old South*. He joined *The New Republic* in 1968 and originated its "Nixon Watch" column in 1969.